Third International Workshop on Natural Language Processing for Social Media

(SocialNLP 2015)

Held at NAACL HLT 2015

Denver, Colorado, USA
5 June 2015

ISBN: 978-1-5108-0433-3

Printed from e-media with permission by:

Curran Associates, Inc.
57 Morehouse Lane
Red Hook, NY 12571

Printed by Curran Associates, Inc. (2015)

For permission requests, please contact the Association for Computational Linguistics at the address below.

Association for Computational Linguistics
209 N. Eighth Street
Stroudsburg, Pennsylvania 18360

Phone: 1-570-476-8006
Fax: 1-570-476-0860

acl@aclweb.org

Additional copies of this publication are available from:

Curran Associates, Inc.
57 Morehouse Lane
Red Hook, NY 12571 USA
Phone: 845-758-0400
Fax: 845-758-2634
Email: curran@proceedings.com
Web: www.proceedings.com

SocialNLP 2015@NAACL Chairs' Welcome

It is our great pleasure to welcome you to the Third Workshop on Natural Language Processing for Social Media – SocialNLP'15, associated with NAACL 2015. SocialNLP is a new inter-disciplinary area of natural language processing (NLP) and social computing. There are three plausible directions of SocialNLP: (1) addressing issues in social computing using NLP techniques; (2) solving NLP problems using information from social media; and (3) handling new problems related to both social computing and natural language processing.

Through this workshop, we anticipate to provide a platform for research outcome presentation and head-to-head discussion in the area of SocialNLP, with the hope to combine the insight and experience of prominent researchers from both NLP and social computing domains to contribute to the area of SocialNLP jointly. Also, selected and expanded versions of papers presented at SocialNLP will be published in two follow-on Special Issues of Springer Cognitive Computation (CogComp) and the International Journal of Computational Linguistics and Chinese Language Processing (IJCLCLP).

The submissions to this year's workshop were again of high quality and we had a competitive selection process. We received 10 submissions from Asia, Europe, and the United States., and due to a rigorous review process, we only accepted 5 of them. Thus the acceptance rate was 50 percent. The workshop papers cover a broad range of SocialNLP-related topics, such as location name disambiguation, microblog and mobile game text processing, product mining, and social media user analysis. We had a total of 27 program committee members, and each submission is evaluated by at least 3 PC members. We warmly thank our PC members for the timely reviews and constructive comments.

We are delighted to have two keynote speeches this year. Prof. Jacob Eisenstein, from Georgia Institute of Technology, will give a talk entitled "Variation and Change in Social Media Language"; Prof. Michael C. Frank, from Stanford University, will give a talk entitled "Predicting Pragmatic Reasoning about Language Use in Context". We also encourage attendees to attend the keynote talk presentations. These valuable and insightful talks can and will guide us to a better understanding of the future.

Putting together SocialNLP 2015 was a team effort. We first thank the authors for providing the content of the program. We are grateful to the program committee members, who worked very hard in reviewing papers and providing feedback for authors. Finally, we especially thank the Workshop Committee Chairs Prof. Matt Post and Prof. Adam Lopez.

We hope you keep supporting SocialNLP workshop and enjoying it!

Organizers of SocialNLP 2015,

Shou-De Lin, Lun-Wei Ku, Cheng-Te Li and Erik Cambria

Organizers:

Shou-de Lin (National Taiwan University, Taiwan)
Lun-Wei Ku (Academia Sinica, Taiwan)
Cheng-Te Li (Academia Sinica, Taiwan)
Erik Cambria (Nanyang Technological University, Singapore)

Program Committee:

Alexandra Balahur (European Commission's Joint Research Centre)
Chia-Hui Chang (National Central University, Taiwan)
Berlin Chen (National Taiwan Normal University, Taiwan)
Hsin-Hsi Chen (National Taiwan University, Taiwan)
Munmun De Choudhury (Georgia Institute of Technology, USA)
Min-Yuh Day (Tamkang University, Taiwan)
Amitava Das (University of North Texas, USA)
Dipankar Das (Jadavpur University, India)
Jennifer Foster (Dublin City University, Ireland)
June-Jei Kuo (National Chung Hsing University, Taiwan)
Chuan-Jie Lin (National Taiwan Ocean University, Taiwan)
Rafal Rzepka (Hokkaido University, Japan)
Yohei Seki (University of Tsukuba, Japan)
Marina Sokolova (University of Ottawa, USA)
Daniela Stockmann (Leiden University, The Netherlands)
Keh-Yih Su (Academia Sinica, Taiwan)
Ming-Feng Tsai (National ChengChi University, Taiwan)
Chi Wang (Microsoft Research, USA)
Hsin-Min Wang (Academia Sinica, Taiwan)
Jenq-Haur Wang (National Taipei University of Technology, Taiwan)
Shih-Hung Wu (Chaoyang University of Technology, Taiwan)
Yejun Wu (Louisiana State University, USA)
Yunqing Xia (Tsinghua University, China)
Ruifeng Xu (Harbin Institute of Technology, China)
Rui Yan (Baidu Inc., China)
Yi-Hsuan Yang (Academia Sinica, Taiwan)
Kevin Zhang (Beijing Institute of Technology, China)

Keynote Speaker:

Jacob Eisenstein (Georgia Institute of Technology, USA)
Michael C. Frank (Stanford University, USA)

Supported by Asia Federation of Natural Language Processing

Keynote Speech (I)

Keynote Speaker (Morning Session):

Jacob Eisenstein (Georgia Institute of Technology, USA)

Title:

Variation and Change in Social Media Language

Abstract:

Social media is sometimes described as a new domain, genre, or task for natural language processing. This suggests that it has specific properties that distinguish it from other sources of text. I will argue that there are exactly two such properties: variation and change. NLP research has historically focused on genres such as newstext, where there is strong pressure towards standardization. Far less pressure exists in social media, and so we must contend with variation on all levels of the linguistic spectrum. This variation enables authors to mark a diverse array of social relationships and identities, and with this increasingly important interpersonal role, online writing becomes enmeshed in complex social processes that lead to instability and change. The inherently dynamic nature of social media language is why we can no longer annotate our way to high accuracy NLP, so learning from unlabeled data will be increasingly critical. Finally, while variation and change pose challenges, they also offer new opportunities for deepening our understanding of both language and social processes. I will describe our recent work on mining four years of Twitter data to uncover macro-scale pathways of linguistic influence among American cities.

Speaker Biography:

Jacob Eisenstein is an Assistant Professor in the School of Interactive Computing at Georgia Tech. He works on statistical natural language processing, focusing on computational sociolinguistics, social media analysis, discourse, and machine learning. He is a recipient of the NSF CAREER Award, a member of the Air Force Office of Scientific Research (AFOSR) Young Investigator Program, and was a SICSA Distinguished Visiting Fellow at the University of Edinburgh. His work has also been supported by the National Institutes for Health, the National Endowment for the Humanities, and Google. Jacob was a Postdoctoral researcher at Carnegie Mellon and the University of Illinois. He completed his Ph.D. at MIT in 2008, winning the George M. Sprowls dissertation award. Jacob's research has been featured in the New York Times, National Public Radio, and the BBC. Thanks to his brief appearance in If These Knishes Could Talk, Jacob has a Bacon number of 2.

Keynote Speech (II)

Keynote Speaker (Afternoon Session):

Michael C. Frank (Stanford University, USA)

Title:

Predicting Pragmatic Reasoning about Language Use in Context

Abstract:

A short, ambiguous message can convey a lot of information, provided the listener is willing to make inferences based on assumptions about the speaker and the context of the message. These sorts of pragmatic inferences are critical in facilitating efficient human communication, and have been characterized informally using tools like Grice's conversational maxims. In this talk, I'll describe our work on a new, probabilistic framework for referential communication in context. This framework shows good fit to adults' and children's judgments across many experiments, provides extensions to a variety of complex linguistic phenomena, and resolves some important puzzles about language processing. I'll end by describing how we have begun to test this framework using data from large-scale corpora of social media conversations.

Speaker Biography:

Michael C. Frank is Associate Professor of Psychology at Stanford University. He earned his BS from Stanford University in Symbolic Systems in 2005 and his PhD from MIT in Brain and Cognitive Sciences in 2010. He studies both adults' language use and children's language learning and how both of these interact with social cognition. His work uses behavioral experiments, computational tools, and novel measurement methods including large-scale web-based studies, eye-tracking, and head-mounted cameras.

Table of Contents

Conference Program

Friday, June 5, 2015

09:20–09:30 ***Opening***

09:30–10:30 ***Keynote Speech (I)***

09:30–10:30 *Variation and Change in Social Media Language*
Jacob Eisenstein (Georgia Institute of Technology)

10:30–11:00 ***Coffee Break (I)***

11:00–12:00 **Natural Language Processing Session**

11:00–11:30 *Location Name Disambiguation Exploiting Spatial Proximity and Temporal Consistency*
Takashi Awamura, Daisuke Kawahara, Eiji ARAMAKI, Tomohide Shibata and Sadao Kurohashi

11:30–12:00 *Paraphrase Identification and Semantic Similarity in Twitter with Simple Features*
Ngoc Phuoc An Vo, Simone Magnolini and Octavian Popescu

12:00–13:30 ***Lunch***

13:30–14:00 ***Panel Discussion***

14:00–15:00 ***Keynote Speech (II)***

14:00–15:00 *Predicting Pragmatic Reasoning about Language Use in Context*
Michael C. Frank (Stanford University)

15:00–15:30 ***Coffee Break (II)***

Friday, June 5, 2015 (continued)

15:30–17:00 Social Media Session

17:00–17:20 *Best Paper Award/Closing*

Location Name Disambiguation Exploiting Spatial Proximity and Temporal Consistency

Takashi Awamura[†] **Eiji Aramaki**[‡] **Daisuke Kawahara**[†]
Tomohide Shibata[†] **Sadao Kurohashi**[†]

[†] Graduate School of Informatics, Kyoto University
[‡] Design School, Kyoto University

awa@nlp.ist.i.kyoto-u.ac.jp, eiji.aramaki@gmail.com,
{dk, shibata, kuro}@i.kyoto-u.ac.jp

Abstract

As the volume of documents on the Web increases, technologies to extract useful information from them become increasingly essential. For instance, information extracted from social network services such as Twitter and Facebook is useful because it contains a lot of location-specific information. To extract such information, it is necessary to identify the location of each location-relevant expression within a document. Previous studies on location disambiguation have tackled this problem on the basis of word sense disambiguation, and did not make use of location-specific clues. In this paper, we propose a method for location disambiguation that takes advantage of the following two clues: spatial proximity and temporal consistency. We confirm the effectiveness of these clues through experiments on Twitter tweets with GPS information.

1 Introduction

As the volume of documents on the Web increases, technologies to extract useful information from them become increasingly essential. For instance, information extracted from social network services (SNS) such as Twitter and Facebook is useful because it contains a lot of location-specific information. To extract such information, it is necessary to identify the location of each location-relevant expression within a document.

However, many previous studies on SNS rely only on geo-tagged documents (e.g., (Han et al., 2013; Han et al., 2014)), which include GPS information, but these represent only a small proportion of the total.[1] To extract as much location information as possible, it is important to develop a method that can estimate locations from numerous documents without GPS information.

Previous studies on location disambiguation made use of methods for word sense disambiguation and are based only on textual information, i.e., the bag-of-words in a document. It is, however, difficult to solve this problem using only textual information in a relatively short SNS document. For example, it is difficult to identify the location of "Prefectural Office Ave." from the following document based only on word information.[2]

> "I arrived at Prefectural Office Ave. from Shuri Station!"

In this paper, we propose a method that identifies the locations of location expressions in Twitter tweets on the basis of the following two clues: (1) spatial proximity, and (2) temporal consistency. Spatial proximity assumes that all locations mentioned in a tweet are close to one another. In the above document, for example, we would assume that "Prefectural Office Ave." is "Prefectural Office Ave. (Okinawa)" using the proximity between "Shuri Station" and "Prefectural Office Ave. (Okinawa)" The other clue is temporal consistency,

[1] Semiocast reported that GPS information is assigned to only 0.77% of all public tweets.

[2] Although it is possible to learn a clue from "Shuri Station," which is located in Okinawa Prefecture, it would require a large amount of training data to learn such lexical clues for each target location expression.

Proceedings of SocialNLP 2015@NAACL-HLT, pages 1–9,
Denver, Colorado, June 5, 2015.

which assumes that the locations in a series of tweets are near to each other.

In our experiments, we learn a location classifier for each ambiguous location expression in Japanese. Hereafter, we call an ambiguous location expression, such as "Prefectural Office Ave.," a **Location EXpression (LEX)**, and a location to which a LEX points, such as <Prefectural Office Ave. (Okinawa)>, a **Location Entity (LE)**, which is linked to its GIS information. We call a LEX linked to multiple LEs an **ambiguous LEX**, which is the target of our location name disambiguation system. That is unambiguous LEXs are not our target, such as "Tokyo Tower," which points the LE <Tokyo Tower>.

We define a set of LEXs and LEs on the basis of Japanese Wikipedia. Training data for the location classifiers are created from tweets containing GPS information. The resulting location classifiers can be applied to LEXs in any tweets or documents without GPS information.

Our novel contributions can be summarized as follows:

- two novel clues for location disambiguation are proposed,
- training data is automatically created from tweets with GPS information, and
- our method can identify LEs of LEXs in any documents without GPS information.

The remainder of this paper is organized as follows. Section 2 introduces related work, while Section 3 describes the resources used in this paper. Section 4 details our proposed method and Section 5 reports the experimental results. Section 6 concludes the paper.

2 Related Work

The location name disambiguation described in this paper is closely connected with Word Sense Disambiguation (WSD), and so studies on WSD are discussed here. We describe studies in location name disambiguation and in the significance of location names in social media.

2.1 Location Estimation

Location name disambiguation has been studied for a long time. It includes estimating one's place of residence and the entity of an ambiguous LEX. Several approaches have been proposed. Although one of the simplest and most reliable is to use IP addresses, many problems can occur, e.g., the IP address of past content cannot be accessed, and this approach is becoming increasingly ineffective with the increased use of portable terminals. As a result, location name disambiguation should now focus on procedures that consider the original text. As information references, Web pages and change logs in Wikipedia have been used as the basis of location name disambiguation. These resources are homogeneous and manageable. In contrast, the numerous data on SNS often contain noise, which makes disambiguation unmanageable.

A number of studies have investigated location name disambiguation. Han et al. (2012) extracted location-indicative words from tweet data by calculating the information gain ratios. Their paper states that the words improved the estimation performance of the users' location. They concluded that the procedure requires relatively little memory, is fast, and could potentially be used by lexicographers to extract location-indicative words. Backstrom et al. (2008) developed a probabilistic framework to quantify the spatial variation manifested in search queries. This allowed them to obtain a measure of spatial dispersion that indicates regional information.

Adams and Janowicz (2012) estimated geographic regions from unstructured, non georeferenced text by computing a probability distribution over the Earth's surface. Their methodology combines natural language processing, geostatistics, and a data-driven bottom-up semantics. Chandra et al. (2011) estimated a city-level user location based purely on a content of tweets, which may include reply-tweet information, without the use of any external information, such as a gazetteer, IP information etc. Chang et al. (2012) proposed two unsupervised methods based on notions of Non-Localness and Geometric-Localness to prune noisy data from tweets. Kinsella et al. (2011) created language models of locations using coordinates extracted from geotagged Twitter data. Van Laere et al. (2014) assigned coordinates to Flickr photos and to Wikipedia articles with Kernel Density Estimation and Ripley's K statistic. Although these studies have estimated location names from location-indicative words or the degree of popularity, most studies neglect spatial proximity, i.e., the distance between two locations, and temporal consistency, i.e., previous tweets from the same user. This paper proposes a new method of location name estimation that considers both spatial proximity and temporal consistency.

2.2 The Importance of Location Name in Social Media

Several researchers have attempted to extract information from SNS such as Twitter. Sakaki et al. (2010) detected earthquakes from tweets containing geographic information system (GIS) information. They judged whether the tweet was posted just after an earthquake using a support vector machine (SVM), and determined the seismic center from the formatted tweets. In addition, they developed a system that raises the alarm about an earthquake from the predicted results. Bollen et al. (2011) extracted the social mood, and predicted the stock price fluctuation N days from the day of observation by using evaluated data of the 'mood-related' dictionary. As a result, they concluded that they could show the 3 days from the 'calm-mood' day might be able to predict the stock price fluctuation. Aramaki et al. (2011) predicted an influenza epidemic from tweets. They showed the possibility of information extraction from the tweets that reflects the actual world's situation by using language processing technologies. Boyd et al. (2010) examined a practice of retweeting as a way by which participants can be "in a conversation." Paul and Dredze (2011) considered a broader range of public health applications for Twitter and showed quantitative correlations with public health data and qualitative evaluations of model output. Baldwin et al. (2013) explored how linguistically noisy or otherwise it is over a range of social media sources empirically over popular social media text types, in the form of YouTube comments, Twitter posts, web user forum posts, blog posts and Wikipedia. Yin et al. (2012) constructed a system architecture for leveraging social media to enhance emergency situation awareness with high-speed text streams retrieved from Twitter during natural disasters and crises.

In these researches, the location of an SNS document plays an important role in extracting information, and in most cases, rely on GPS function connected to the tweets. However, in fact, there are less than 1% of the entire tweets that are connected to GPS. In order to enhance the accuracy of such research, it is necessary to use the framework that enables to discriminate the location out of the texts and words of the tweets that do not contain GPS information.

3 Resources

3.1 LEX Database

First, it is necessary to define the LEXs and LEs handled in this study. We focus on LEXs and LEs that have GIS information on Wikipedia. In this paper, we call the database of LEXs and LEs **LEX database**, and use two methods to obtain the LEX database from Wikipedia according to the type of GIS data:

- Infobox
- Latitude/longitude information

3.1.1 Infobox

The Infobox is a meta-template on a Wikipedia page (as shown in Figure 1). Infobox, which the article of a location name has, sometimes contains its address and latitude/longitude. We extract entries that have such Infoboxes as LEs.

We ran this process on the Japanese Wikipedia, and extracted 759 LEXs and 884 LEs as a result.

3.1.2 Latitude/Longitude Information

The latitude/longitude information is often given at the top of a Wikipedia article about a location (as shown in Figure 2). We extract LEs and LEXs from Wikipedia articles that contain such GIS information. We extracted 17,140 LEXs and 17,426 LEs by applying this method to the Japanese Wikipedia.

We merged these two databases to generate our LEX database, deleting duplicate LEs in the process. In total, we obtained 17,724 LEXs and 18,256 LEs. Table 1 lists the LEs of "Prefectural Office Ave." Table 2 lists the frequencies of LEXs and LEs according to the number of LEs for a LEX. From this table, we can see that we have 462 ambiguous LEXs, which correspond to 994 LEs.

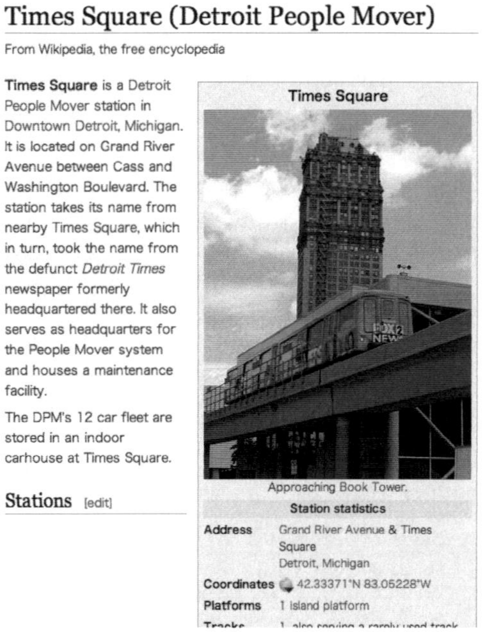

Figure 1: Infobox information

ID	LE	Lat	Long
1	Prefectural Office Ave. (Hyogo)	34.69	135.18
2	Prefectural Office Ave. (Chiba)	35.60	140.12
3	Prefectural Office Ave. (Toyama)	36.69	137.20
4	Prefectural Office Ave. (Hiroshima)	34.39	132.45
5	Prefectural Office Ave. (Ehime)	33.84	132.76
6	Prefectural Office Ave. (Kohchi)	33.55	133.53
7	Prefectural Office Ave. (Okinawa)	26.21	127.67

Table 1: LEs for the LEX "Prefectural Office Ave."

In this study, a location name with parenthesis is used for an LE, such as <Times Square (Detroit People Mover)> and <Times Square (Hong Kong)> shown in Figure 1, 2, and a string without the part in brackets is used for a LEX, such as "Times Square."

3.2 Corpus for Location Name Disambiguation

The disambiguation of LEXs requires a corpus in which each LEX is assigned to an LE. We extract this from Twitter data with GIS information. For example, given a tweet "Let's meet at the Prefectural Office Ave." that has GIS latitude and longitude information indicating Okinawa, it is natural that the "Prefectural Office Ave." in the tweet indicates the LE <Prefectural Office Ave. (Okinawa)>. Therefore, we assign LEs to LEXs in tweets based on their GIS information using the following method.

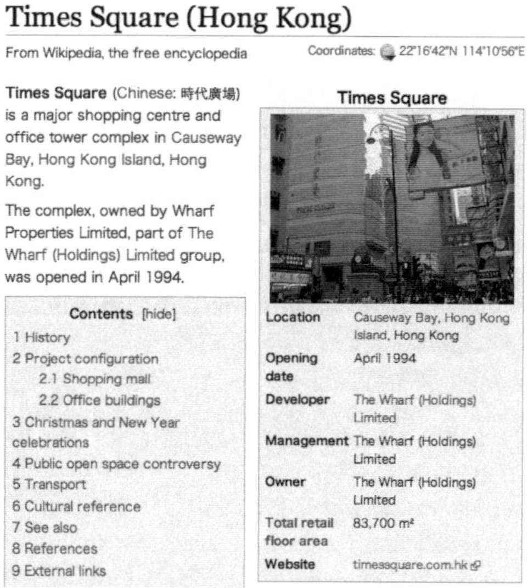

Figure 2: Latitude/longitude information

# of LEs	LEX	LE
1	17,262	17,262
2	412	824
3	38	114
4	8	32
5	2	10
7	2	14
Sum	17,724	18,256

Table 2: Statistics of LEX database

- STEP 0 (pre-processing): Preparation of tweets

  We obtained tweet data containing GIS information from 2011/7/15 to 2012/7/31. We removed duplicate tweets.

- STEP 1: Extraction of tweets including LEXs

  Tweets including ambiguous LEXs are extracted based on the LEX database described in Section 3.1. Tweets including unambiguous LEXs are not used for our target tweets but used for the clues of temporal consistency described in Section 4.3. This process searches for LEX strings within a tweet, and aggregates such tweets for each LEX. If several ambiguous LEXs are included in a tweet, this tweet is used for each LEX. For example, "I'll go to Motomachi station from Prefectural Office Ave." is used for "Motomachi station" and "Prefectural Office Ave."

- STEP 2: Assignment of LEs

  An LE is assigned to tweets for each LEX extracted in STEP 1. This process is conducted on the basis of the GIS information in the tweet and the LEs of the target LEX. Our idea is that if the distance between the tweet GIS and an LE GIS is short, the LEX in the tweet may point to this LE. For example, if the GIS of the tweet including "Prefectural Office Ave." is near <Prefectural Office Ave. (Okinawa)>, this "Prefectural Office Ave." may point to <Prefectural Office Ave. (Okinawa)>. In this paper, we set the distance threshold for the judgment of LEs to 10km. That is, if the distance between the tweet GIS and an LE GIS is less than 10 km, this LE is assigned to the tweet; otherwise this tweet is discarded. If the distance of several LEs is less than 10 km, the LE with the shortest distance is assigned to the tweet.

Approximately 180,000 tweets including ambiguous LEXs were obtained. Out of 462 ambiguous LEXs in the LEX database, 353 contain at least one tweet. We employed them as the gold standard data used in our experiments.

One of our novel contributions of this study is that we automatically constructed this large-scale corpus with GIS information, whereas previous studies on toponym resolution created a corpus by hand (Leidner, 2008).

4 Method for Location Name Disambiguation

We propose a method for location name disambiguation in tweets. Our approach automatically distinguishes LEs for a LEX in a tweet using a machine learning algorithm: SVM. The SVM classifiers are generated for each LEX. Each SVM classifier has the following features.

4.1 Baseline Features

We use the following two features as baseline features:

(1) Lexical feature: bag of words in the tweet

(2) Majority feature: frequency of LEs

4.2 Spatial Proximity Features

The distance between a target ambiguous LEX and an unambiguous LEX in the tweets is used for the spatial proximity features. An example is shown below.

Figure 3: Locations of "Prefectural Office Ave." in Japan

(1) It takes about 20 minutes to get from Shuri station to Prefectural Office Ave.

The ambiguous LEX "Prefectural Office Ave." has seven LEs (shown in Figure 3).

In this example, it is difficult to estimate the LE based only on the lexical information. However, the relation between the LEX and other unambiguous locations in the same text provides a clue for the disambiguation of the LEX. In general, related LEXs tend to exist alongside the target LEX. Although the words in tweets may be learned implicitly from this relation by SVM, they cannot also be expected to occur. Thus, our method explicitly uses the distance between two locations as the relation. We assume that the distances between the LE of the target LEX and other LEs are short. For example, in the above example of "Prefectural Office Ave.," <Shuri station> is relatively close to <Prefectural Office Ave. (Okinawa)>, but is not near <Prefectural Office Ave. (Chiba)> Thus, it can be estimated that the LE of "Prefectural Office Ave." is <Prefectural Office Ave. (Okinawa)>

To assign the spatial proximity features to a tweet, we first check whether the tweet includes LEXs. If the LEXs are unambiguous, we then calculate the distance between the unambiguous LE and each target LE.[3] Features depending on the distance are assigned to the tweet. If the LEXs are ambiguous, spatial proximity features are not used, because the LEs

[3]If there are multiple unambiguous LEs in the tweet, all of these are considered as features.

indicated by the LEXs cannot be determined.

For example, when a tweet with "Prefectural Office Ave." contains the unambiguous LEX "Shuri Station," the distance between <Shuri Station> and each LE indicating "Prefectural Office Ave." is calculated. If the distance between <Shuri Station> and <Prefectural Office Ave. (Okinawa)> is 0∼10 km and that between <Shuri Station> and <Prefectural Office Ave. (Chiba)> is 500∼1,000 km, these distances are used as different features. The number of spatial consistency features is ld, where l is the number of LEs for the target LEX and d is the number of distance bins, which are described in Section 5.

4.3 Temporal Consistency Features

Until now, we have considered only a single target tweet to estimate locations. However, the target tweet sometimes contains few useful clues for LEX disambiguation because the tweet is too short. Therefore, this paper considers the preceding tweets posted in the previous t hours. The baseline features and the spatial proximity features are also extracted from these preceding tweets. An example is shown below.

(2) I arrived at the Prefectural Office Ave.

Its preceding tweets are as follows:

(3) I'm going to take an airplane. I'm looking forward to Okinawa!

(4) I arrived in Okinawa!

(5) I'm heading for Shuri Station by Yui Rail.

In such a case, useful information for location estimation can be obtained by considering these preceding tweets. For example, "Okinawa" is related to <Prefectural Office Ave. (Okinawa)>, and <Shuri Station> is near <Prefectural Office Ave. (Okinawa)> Based on such information, it can be estimated that the LE of "Prefectural Office Ave." is <Prefectural Office Ave. (Okinawa)>

It is necessary to determine the time threshold t. This is because extremely old tweets are hardly related to the target tweet. We will discuss this issue in Section 5.

Method	Settings
Sp (0∼10, 100∼500 km)	+10∼100 km
	+10∼50, 50∼100 km
	+10∼100, 500∼1000 km
	+10∼50, 50∼100, 500∼1000 km
Ts	Indefinite
	∼24 h
	∼12 h
	∼6 h
	∼3 h
	∼1 h

Table 3: Settings for Sp and Ts

5 Experiments and Discussion

5.1 Experimental Settings

We create an SVM classifier for each LEX to solve location name disambiguation with the features described in Section 4. This classifier identifies the LE for an ambiguous LEX included in a tweet. Since location name disambiguation is a multi-class identification problem, we use the one-versus-the-rest method for the SVM classifier. For the gold-standard data, we used 70,184 tweets including the LEXs that are associated with ten or more tweets from the corpus described in Section 3.2. We conducted 5-fold cross-validation using this data. We adopted TinySVM,[4] an SVM package with a quadratic polynomial kernel. For the segmentation of Japanese words, we used the Japanese morphological analyzer JUMAN.[5]

5.2 Methods for Comparison

We compare the following four methods in this study:

- Baseline (B): This method uses only the following two features: (1) lexical features, and (2) majority features. We used the base form of words in a tweet as SVM features. Here, we used only high-frequency words (top 100,000). We regard the frequency of a word in a tweet as the lexical feature.
- +Spatial Proximity (+Sp): This method uses the baseline features and the spatial proximity features. The spatial proximity features are generated from the distance between the target LE and another unambiguous LEX (LE)

[4]http://chasen.org/~taku/software/TinySVM/

[5]http://nlp.ist.i.kyoto-u.ac.jp/index.php?JUMAN

mentioned in the same tweet (as described in Section 4.2). We examined four sets of distance bins as listed in Table 3 (default: 0∼10, 100∼500 km). Each feature of spatial proximity is considered separately according to the distance bins. The values are the number of LEs in the same tweet that satisfy the distance condition.

- +Temporal Consistency (+TC): This method uses baseline features and temporal consistency features. The temporal consistency features are generated from recent tweets (maximum of three), as described in Section 4.3. This feature disregards non-recent tweets. We investigated six definitions of recency as listed in Table 3.
- +Spatial Proximity +Temporal Consistency (+SP+TC): This method uses all features, i.e., baseline, spatial proximity, and temporal consistency features. The spatial proximity features are also generated from the preceding tweets that are used to generate the temporal consistency features.

5.3 Evaluation

The accuracy $\frac{s}{c}$ is calculated from the system output and the correct LEs, where s is the number of tweets whose output had the correct LE and c is the total number of tweets considered. Moreover, the accuracy is calculated separately for each number of tweets per LEX (10∼100: rare LEX, 100∼1,000: intermediate LEX, 1,000∼: common LEX, 10∼: all).

5.4 Experimental Results and Discussions

The results for all methods are compared in Table 4 with the following proximity and consistency features:

- 0∼10, 10∼100, 100∼500 km
- ∼6 h

The Majority Baseline (MB) is a baseline method that outputs the most frequent LE for each LEX.

Table 4 lists the accuracy of the estimated LEs considering spatial proximity and temporal consistency. In particular, considering the proximity improves the accuracy, regardless of the number of tweets for each LEX. Although the consideration of temporal consistency also improves accuracy forrare LEXs. the accuracy is below the baseline for common LEXs.The accuracy considering both features outperforms the baseline by 7.13% for rare LEXs.In addition, a sign-test was adopted to demonstrate the significance of the results. This test was performed using R.[6] "†" means the superiority to B estimated at a significance level of 5%, and "‡" means that at the 1% level. This test shows the significance of the proposed method, particularly for rare LEXs.Moreover, the accuracy with all tweets verifies the significance of the proposed method compared to the baseline.

The accuracy did not improve for common LEXsbecause of an imbalance in the tweet data. This study only uses tweet data that include LEXs and GIS information. Therefore, the LEs of the tweets are imbalanced for each LEX. The high accuracy of MB suggests this imbalance depends on the number of tweets for each LEX. Moreover, most tweets with GIS information are generated automatically by companies such as Foursquare. As a result, high accuracy is obtained in many cases without considering the proximity or consistency. Although this study used only tweets with GIS information, the accuracy could clearly be improved using tweets with-

# of Tweets (Sum)	Method	# of Correct	Accuracy
10∼100 (4,891)	MB	4,171	0.8528
	B	4,485	0.9170
	+SP	4,515	0.9231 ‡
	+TC	4,491	0.9182 ‡
	+SP+TC	**4,520**	**0.9241** ‡
100∼1000 (25,758)	MB	22,477	0.8726
	B	24,725	0.9599
	+SP	**24,752**	**0.9609**
	+TC	24,708	0.9592
	+SP+TC	24,737	0.9604
1000∼ (39,535)	MB	36,896	0.9332
	B	39,041	0.9875
	+SP	**39,054**	**0.9878**
	+TC	39,036	0.9874
	+SP+TC	**39,054**	**0.9878**
10∼ (70,184)	MB	63,544	0.9054
	B	68,251	0.9725
	+SP	**68,321**	**0.9735** ‡
	+TC	68,235	0.9722
	+SP+TC	68,311	0.9733 †

"†" means the superiority to B estimated at the 5% significance level and "‡" means that at the 1% level.

Table 4: Main results

[6] http://cran.r-project.org/

# of Tweets (Sum)	Proximity	# of Correct	Accuracy
	+10∼100 km	4,515	0.9231
10∼100	+10∼50, 50∼100 km	4,513	0.9227
(4,891)	+10∼100, 500∼1000 km	4,519	0.9239
	+10∼50, 50∼100, 500∼1000 km	**4,520**	**0.9241**
	+10∼100 km	24,752	0.9599
100∼1000	**+10∼50, 50∼100 km**	**24,758**	**0.9612**
(25,758)	+10∼100, 500∼1000 km	24,744	0.9606
	+10∼50, 50∼100, 500∼1000 km	24,746	0.9607
	+10∼100 km	39,053	0.9878
1000∼	**+10∼50, 50∼100 km**	**39,069**	**0.9882**
(39,535)	+10∼100, 500∼1000 km	39,064	0.9881
	+10∼50, 50∼100, 500∼1000 km	39,065	0.9881

Table 5: Comparison of SP features

# of Tweets (Sum)	Terms	# of Correct	Accuracy
	indefinite	4,429	0.9055
	∼24 h	4,491	0.9182
10∼100	∼12 h	4,493	0.9186
(4,891)	∼6 h	4,491	0.9182
	∼3 h	**4,494**	**0.9188**
	∼1 h	4,493	0.9186
	indefinite	24,694	0.9587
	∼24 h	24,700	0.9589
100∼1,000	∼12 h	24,709	0.9593
(25,758)	∼6 h	24,708	0.9592
	∼3 h	24,718	0.9596
	∼1 h	**24,725**	**0.9599**
	indefinite	38,988	0.9862
	∼24 h	38,988	0.9873
1,000∼	**∼12 h**	**39,036**	**0.9874**
(39,535)	**∼6 h**	**39,036**	**0.9874**
	∼3 h	39,033	0.9873
	∼1 h	39,034	0.9873

Table 6: Comparison of TC features

out GIS information.

A comparison of the results for various proximity levels is shown in Table 5. As shown in Table 5, the accuracy of location name disambiguation with rare LEXs improves with the addition of the 500∼1000 km bin. However, when many tweets are considered, the accuracy improves with the addition of 10∼50 and 50∼100 km bins. This implies that the LE estimation requires additional information when there are few tweets, and less information when many tweets are available.

A comparison of the results for different degrees of temporal consistency is shown in Table 6. Although there were few remarkable results, it is clear that the accuracy does not improve significantly when older tweets are considered. In particular, the poorest accuracy was achieved when specific terms are not defined. This shows the validity of considering specific terms.

6 Conclusions and Future Work

In this paper, we presented a method for location name disambiguation for text snippets on SNS. We considered both the spatial proximity and temporal consistency to produce the estimates of LEs. As a result, our method substantially outperformed the baseline method that considers only lexical information. More specifically:

- Considering the spatial proximity improves the accuracy
- Considering the temporal consistency with many tweets improves the accuracy
- Considering both of the above outperforms the baseline by 7.13%

In future work, first, we plan to further investigate the cause of the decrease in accuracy when the temporal consistency feature considers many tweets.

Second, in this paper, only tweets including unambiguous LEXs are used to calculate the proximity feature for the target LEX. However, tweets including ambiguous LEXs could also be used if the LEXs have been disambiguated in advance.

In addition, we estimated the LEs of ambiguous LEXs, although the location estimation has several problems. One concerns whether the user posting the tweet including the LEX is actually at that location. Solving this problem is necessary for some applications specializing in GIS information. In future work, we aim to solve this problem using the proposed spatial proximity and temporal consistency.

References

Benjamin Adams and Krzysztof Janowicz. 2012. On the geo-indicativeness of non-georeferenced text. In John G. Breslin, Nicole B. Ellison, James G. Shanahan, and Zeynep Tufekci, editors, *ICWSM*. The AAAI Press.

Eiji Aramaki, Sachiko Maskawa, and Mizuki Morita. 2011. Twitter catches the flu: Detecting influenza epidemics using twitter. In *Proceedings of the Conference on Empirical Methods in Natural Language Processing*, EMNLP '11, pages 1568–1576, Stroudsburg, PA, USA. Association for Computational Linguistics.

Lars Backstrom, Jon Kleinberg, Ravi Kumar, and Jasmine Novak. 2008. Spatial variation in search engine queries. In *Proceedings of the 17th International Conference on World Wide Web*, WWW '08, pages 357–366, New York, NY, USA. ACM.

Timothy Baldwin, Paul Cook, Marco Lui, Andrew Mackinlay, and Li Wang. 2013. How noisy social media text, how diffrnt social media sources?

J. Bollen, H. Mao, and X. Zeng. 2011. Twitter mood predicts the stock market. *Journal of Computational Science*, pages 1–8.

Danah Boyd, Scott Golder, and Gilad Lotan. 2010. Tweet, tweet, retweet: Conversational aspects of retweeting on twitter. In *Proceedings of the 2010 43rd Hawaii International Conference on System Sciences*, HICSS '10, pages 1–10, Washington, DC, USA. IEEE Computer Society.

S. Chandra, L. Khan, and F.B. Muhaya. 2011. Estimating twitter user location using social interactions–a content based approach. In *Privacy, security, risk and trust (passat), 2011 IEEE third international conference on and 2011 IEEE third international conference on social computing (socialcom)*, pages 838–843, Oct.

Hau-wen Chang, Dongwon Lee, Mohammed Eltaher, and Jeongkyu Lee. 2012. @phillies tweeting from philly? predicting twitter user locations with spatial word usage. In *Proceedings of the 2012 International Conference on Advances in Social Networks Analysis and Mining (ASONAM 2012)*, ASONAM '12, pages 111–118, Washington, DC, USA. IEEE Computer Society.

Bo Han, Paul Cook, and Timothy Baldwin. 2012. Geolocation prediction in social media data by finding location indicative words. In *Proceedings of COLING 2012*, pages 1045–1062, December.

Bo Han, Paul Cook, and Timothy Baldwin. 2013. A stacking-based approach to twitter user geolocation prediction. In *Proceedings of the 51st Annual Meeting of the Association for Computational Linguistics: System Demonstrations*, pages 7–12, Sofia, Bulgaria, August. Association for Computational Linguistics.

Bo Han, Paul Cook, and Timothy Baldwin. 2014. Text-based twitter user geolocation prediction. *J. Artif. Intell. Res. (JAIR)*, 49:451–500.

Sheila Kinsella, Vanessa Murdock, and Neil O'Hare. 2011. "I ' m Eating a Sandwich in Glasgow '' : Modeling locations with tweets. In *Proceedings of the 3rd International Workshop on Search and Mining User-generated Contents*, SMUC '11, pages 61–68, New York, NY, USA. ACM.

Jochen L Leidner. 2008. *Toponym Resolution in Text : Annotation, Evaluation and Applications of Spatial Grounding of Place Names*. Universal Press, Boca Raton, FL, USA.

Michael Paul and Mark Dredze. 2011. You are what you tweet : Analyzing twitter for public health. In *5th Interational Conference on Weblogs and Social Media*, pages 265–272. AAAI Press.

Takeshi Sakaki, Makoto Okazaki, and Yutaka Matsuo. 2010. Earthquake shakes twitter users: Real-time event detection by social sensors. In *Proceedings of the 19th International Conference on World Wide Web*, WWW '10, pages 851–860, New York, NY, USA. ACM.

Olivier Van Laere, Jonathan Quinn, Steven Schockaert, and Bart Dhoedt. 2014. Spatially aware term selection for geotagging. *IEEE Trans. on Knowl. and Data Eng.*, 26(1):221–234, January.

Jie Yin, A. Lampert, M. Cameron, B. Robinson, and R. Power. 2012. Using social media to enhance emergency situation awareness. *Intelligent Systems, IEEE*, 27(6):52–59, Nov.

Paraphrase Identification and Semantic Similarity in Twitter with Simple Features

Ngoc Phuoc An Vo
Fondazione Bruno Kessler,
University of Trento
Trento, Italy
ngoc@fbk.eu

Simone Magnolini
University of Brescia,
Fondazione Bruno Kessler
Trento, Italy
magnolini@fbk.eu

Octavian Popescu
IBM Research, T.J. Watson
Yorktown, US
o.popescu@us.ibm.com

Abstract

Paraphrase Identification and Semantic Similarity are two different yet well related tasks in NLP. There are many studies on these two tasks extensively on structured texts in the past. However, with the strong rise of social media data, studying these tasks on unstructured texts, particularly, social texts in Twitter is very interesting as it could be more complicated problems to deal with. We investigate and find a set of simple features which enables us to achieve very competitive performance on both tasks in Twitter data. Interestingly, we also confirm the significance of using word alignment techniques from evaluation metrics in machine translation in the overall performance of these tasks.

1 Introduction

Paraphrase Identification and Semantic Similarity are important tasks that can be used as features to improve many other Natural Language Processing (NLP) tasks, e.g. Information Retrieval, Machine Translation Evaluation, Text Summarization, Question and Answering, and others. Besides this, analyzing social media data like tweets of the social network Twitter is a field of growing interest for different purposes. The study of these typical NLP tasks on Twitter data can be very interesting as social media data carries lot of surprises and unpredictable information.

The Paraphrase Identification is a classic NLP task which is a classification problem. Given a pair of sentences, the system is required to assess if the two sentences carry the same meaning, to classify them *paraphrase*, or *not paraphrase* otherwise. Likewise, Semantic Similarity is another NLP task in which the system needs to examine the similarity degree (in a pre-defined semantic scale) of a given pair of texts, varying in different levels such as word, phrase, sentence, or paragraph.

There are different approaches, both supervised and unsupervised, have been proposed for these two tasks, ranging from simple level like word/n-gram overlapping, string matching, to more complicated ones like semantic word similarity, word alignment, syntactic structure, etc.[1,2] However, it is challenging or even inapplicable to deploy all these approaches to social media data, like Twitter data, due to many differences the social media data carries, such as misspelling, word out of vocabulary, slang, acronyms, style, structure, etc. In this paper, we study and find a set of simple features specifically chosen and suitable for social media data which is relatively easy to obtain, but able to achieve very competitive performance on both tasks for Twitter data. We also analyze the significance of each feature quantitatively and qualitatively in the overall performance. As a result, we can prove our hypothesis that the combination of simple features like word/n-gram overlapping, word alignment, and semantic word similarity can result in very good performance for both tasks on social media data.

The paper is organized as follows: Section 2

[1] http://aclweb.org/aclwiki/index.php?title=Paraphrase_Identification_(State_of_the_art)

[2] http://aclweb.org/aclwiki/index.php?title=Similarity_(State_of_the_art)

Proceedings of SocialNLP 2015@NAACL-HLT, pages 10–19,
Denver, Colorado, June 5, 2015.

presents the Related Work, Section 3 describes the tasks and set of features, Section 4 shows the Experiments, Section 5 reports the Evaluations, Section 6 discusses the Error Analysis, and finally Section 7 is the Conclusions and Future Work.

2 Related Work

The ability to identify paraphrase, in which a sentences express the same meaning of another one but with different words, has proven useful for a wide variety of natural language processing applications (Madnani and Dorr, 2010). The ACL Wiki gives an excellent summary of the state-of-the-art paraphrase identification techniques; this shows how much effort researchers did to automatically detecting paraphrases.[3] The different approaches can be categorized into supervised methods, i.e. (Madnani et al., 2012), (Socher et al., 2011) and (Wan et al., 2006), that, at the moment, are the most promising and unsupervised methods, i.e. (Fernando and Stevenson, 2008), (Hassan and Adviser-Mihalcea, 2011) and (Islam and Inkpen, 2009). Previous works use the Microsoft Research Paraphrase Corpus (MSRP) dataset (Dolan et al., 2004) that is obtained by extracting sentences from news sources on the web; however, this scenario is very different from social data. A few recent studies have highlighted the potentiality and importance of developing paraphrase (Zanzotto et al., 2011) and (Xu et al., 2013) and semantic similarity techniques (Guo and Diab, 2012) specifically for Tweets. They also indicated that the very informal language, especially the high degree of lexical variation, used in social media has posed serious challenges. Twitter data and, more in general, social media data have been used as dataset in a growing topic of research. Twitter, at the moment the most used microblogging tool, has seen a lot of growth since it launched in October, 2006. In (Java et al., 2007) preliminary analysis they find user clusters based on user intention to topics by clique percolation methods. This research is expanded and improved in several ways in (Krishnamurthy et al., 2008), they applied geographical characterization to cluster users and also found relation between the number of following and followers of a user. These and other similar researches have helped to obtain a more precise idea about some effect that action in this microblogging platform can have; (Kwak et al., 2010) use previous works as a base to rank users adding the effect of retweets on information propagation. With the data obtained from the population of blogs and social networks, opinion mining and sentiment analysis became, in the last years, a field of interest for many researches. In the literature (Pak and Paroubek, 2010), they describe a method for an automatic collection of a corpus that can be used to train a sentiment classifier. In a further research (Kouloumpis et al., 2011), it shows that part-of-speech features may not be useful for sentiment analysis in the microblogging domain, instead using hash-tags to collect training data did prove useful, as did using data collected based on positive and negative emoticons.

3 Paraphrase and Semantic Similarity in Twitter

In this section, we introduce the two tasks Paraphrase Identification and Semantic Similarity in Twitter, then we describe the set of simple features which enables us to achieve competitive performance in both tasks.

3.1 Task Description

This is a shared-task proposed as the Task#1 "Paraphrase and Semantic Similarity in Twitter" at SemEval 2015 (Xu et al., 2015).[4] In this task, the first common ground for development and comparison of Paraphrase Identification (PI) and Semantic Similarity (SS) systems for the Twitter data is provided. Given a pair of sentences from Twitter trends, systems are required to produce a binary *yes/no* judgment and an optionally graded similarity score in the scale [0-1] to measure their semantic equivalence. This task is used to promote this line of research in the new challenging setting of social media data, and help to advance other NLP techniques for noisy user-generated text in the long run. Figure 1 shows examples of paraphrase and non-paraphrase pairs in Twitter.

[3] http://aclweb.org/aclwiki/index.php?title=Paraphrase_Identification_%28State_of_the_art%29

[4] http://alt.qcri.org/semeval2015/task1/

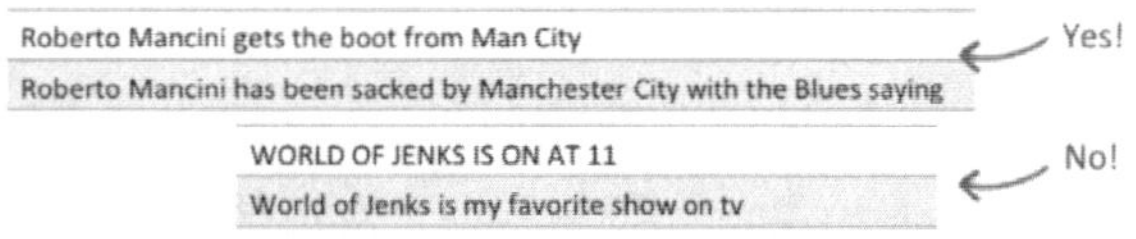

Figure 1: Examples of PI in Twitter.

3.2 Data Preprocessing

In order to optimize the system performance, we carefully analyze the dataset and notice that Tweets' topic is a part that is always present in both sentences; this redundant similarity in the pairs does not give any information about paraphrase as two sentences always have the same topic, yet they may be paraphrase or not. Hence, we remove the topic from the sentences, and we did the same in the pairs with Part-of-Speech (POS) and named entity tags. As being suggested by the guideline of the task, we also remove all the pairs with uncertain judgment, such as "debatable" since they cannot confirm the *paraphrase/not paraphrase* relation between two sentences. After this data processing, we obtain two smaller datasets with very short texts, sometime reduced to a single word and with very poor syntactic structure. We split the original dataset into two subsets, in which one is composed by sentence pairs and the other one is composed by pairs with POS and named entity tags.

As Twitter data and other micro-blog data are usually informal text which is quite short in length and written in a variety of noise of presentation, e.g *"coooooool"* v.s *"cool"*, *"talkin"* v.s *"talking"*, *"u"* v.s *"you"*, *"thinkin"* v.s *"thinking"*, *"abt"* v.s *"about"*, etc. We apply the lexical normalization method (Han et al., 2013) to normalize noisy lexical from the input data. We also notice the simple structure of given datasets, especially, after undergoing the preprocessing, we decide to focus on exploiting the lexical and string similarity information, rather than syntactic information.

3.3 Feature Set

In order to build the system, we investigate and extract a set of simple features especially tailored for social media data which can be used for both tasks, for building either a binary classifier for detecting paraphrase or regression model to compute the similarity scores on Twitter data. Moreover, these features can be used independently or together with others to measure the semantic similarity and recognize the paraphrase of given sentence pair as well as to evaluate the significance of each feature to the accuracy of system's predictions. On top of this, the system is expandable and scalable for adopting more useful features aiming for improving the accuracy.

Lexical and String Similarity. We use the system described in the literature (Das and Smith, 2009) to compute the lexical and string similarity between two sentences by using a logistic regression model with eighteen features based on n-grams. This system uses precision, recall and F1-score of 1-gram, 2-gram and 3-gram of tokens and stems from sentence pair to build a binary classification model for identifying paraphrase. We extract the eighteen features from this system to use in our classification model.

Machine Translation Evaluation Metrics. Other than similarity features, we also use evaluation metrics in machine translation as suggested in (Madnani et al., 2012) for paraphrase recognition on Microsoft Research paraphrase corpus (MSRP) (Dolan et al., 2004). In machine translation, the evaluation metric scores the hypotheses by aligning them to one or more reference translations. We take into consideration to use all the eight metrics proposed, but we find that adding some of them without a careful process of training on the dataset may decrease the performance of the system. Thus, we only use two metrics in our system, the METEOR and BLEU. We actually also take into consideration the metric TERp (Snover et al., 2009), but it does not make any improvement on system performance, hence, we exclude it.

METEOR (Metric for Evaluation of Translation with Explicit ORdering). We use the latest version of METEOR (Denkowski and Lavie, 2014) that find alignments between sentences based on exact, stem, synonym and paraphrase matches between words and phrases. We used the system as distributed on its website using only the "norm" option that tokenizes and normalizes punctuation and lowercase as suggested by documentation.[5] We compute the word alignment scores on sentences and on sentences with part-of-speech and named entity tags, as our idea is

[5]http://www.cs.cmu.edu/ alavie/METEOR/index.html

Classifier/Features	Word/ n-grams Overlap (1)	(1) +METEOR	(1) +METEOR +TERp	(1) +METEOR +BLEU	(1) +METEOR +BLEU +EditDistance
Baseline-1	72.4	-	-	-	-
EditDistance	73.3	-	-	-	-
Decision Stump	73.7	74.4	74.4	74.4	74.4
OneR	73.7	74.4	74.4	74.4	74.4
Logistic	73.6	74.9	74.9	74.9	75.0
J48	72.6	74.7	74.2	74.6	74.7
BaysianLogisticRegression	72.0	74.9	74.8	74.9	75.0
VotedPerceptron	73.7	75.6	75.5	75.8	**76.2**
MultiLayerPerceptron	73.9	75.6	75.3	75.4	76.1

Table 1: Paraphrase Identification Accuracy (%) obtained using different classifiers with different features on Development data.

that if two sentences are similar, their tagged version also should be similar.

BLEU (Bilingual Evaluation Understudy). We use another metric for machine translation BLEU (Papineni et al., 2002) that is one of the most commonly used and because of that has an high reliability. It is computed as the amount of n-gram overlap, for different values of n=1,2,3, and 4, between the system output and the reference translation, in our case between sentence pairs. The score is tempered by a penalty for translations that might be too short. BLEU relies on exact matching and has no concept of synonymy or paraphrasing. As the length of tweets is relatively short, it is only 140-character message, we do not expect to have large n-gram overlaps, except 1-gram and 2-gram. Our analysis actually shows that 3-gram, 4-gram and the average score may cause more noise.

Edit Distance. We use the edit distance between sentences as a feature. For that we used the Excitement Open Platform (EOP) (Magnini et al., 2014).[6] To obtain the edit distance, we use EDITS Entailment Decision Algorithm (EDITS EDA) taking the edit distance instead of entailment or not entailment decision. We configure the system to use lemmas and synonyms as identical words to compute sentence distance, the system normalizes the score on the number of token of the shortest sentence. We choose this configuration because it returns the best performance evaluated on training and development data.

[6]http://hltfbk.github.io/Excitement-Open-Platform/

Sentiment Analysis. We speculate to improve paraphrase detection by adding a feature based on polarity given by a sentiment analysis system. We evaluate this feature on all three datasets (training, develpment, and testing). We use the Sentiment Pipeline of Stanford CoreNLP (Manning et al., 2014) to obtain this feature. We configure the pipeline for tokenizing, splitting sentence, POS tagging, lemmatization , parsing, named entity recognition (NER) and, of course, sentiment analysis. Despite the deep analysis, most of sentences are classified as either *"positive"*, *"negative"* or *"neutral"*; classes *"very positive"* and *"very negative"* are rare. We decide to use this as a polarity-matching feature (i.e. when both sentences in the pair are classified the same class), so we analyze the distribution of paraphrase and polarity matching on the three datasets, which results are shown in Table 2, Table 3 and Table 4. Contrary to our intuition, this feature seems not to be strongly correlated with paraphrasing, in particular, pairs with polarity matching have 2.08% more of probability to be paraphrase in the training dataset, a bit more (3.65%) in the development dataset, but even less (1.76%) in the test dataset. We also compute the information gain of the feature in the training dataset using WEKA (Hall et al., 2009) InfoGainAttributeEval with the default ranker and we obtain a low result, only 0.00107, so we decide to exclude this approach. We still think that sentiment analysis could be an useful feature for paraphrase detection, and there would be a way to use it properly. To prove that, we try another different approach, instead of using a binary feature, we use three possible values: 0 if the polarity is opposite ("positive" and "negative"), 0.5 if one or both sentences in the pair are classified as "neutral" and 1 if they have the same polarity (both "positive" or "negative"). We compute the information gain of the feature in the training dataset and obtain a more promising score of 0.01272; this seems to confirm our idea on the sentiment analysis. Probably a wider range of values (more than just a 3 sub-classes) would possibly obtain better results. We aim to use a continuous value that describes polarity distance to improve our system performance.

	Paraphrase	Not Paraphrase
Without Sent. An.	3996 / 11530 34.66 %	7534 / 11530 65.34 %
Match	1856 / 5052 36.74 %	3196 / 5052 63.26 %
Mismatch	2140 / 6478 33.03 %	4338 / 6478 66.97 %

Table 2: Distribution of the paraphrase in training dataset without sentiment analysis and with polarity matching and mismatching.

	Paraphrase	Not Paraphrase
Without Sent. An.	1470 / 4142 35.49 %	2672 / 4142 64.51 %
Match	750 / 1916 39.14 %	1166 / 1916 60.86 %
Mismatch	720 / 2226 32.35 %	1506 / 2226 67.65 %

Table 3: Distribution of the paraphrase in development dataset without sentiment analysis and with polarity matching and mismatching.

	Paraphrase	Not Paraphrase
Without Sent. An.	175 / 838 20.88 %	663 / 838 79.12 %
Match	84 / 371 22.64 %	287 / 371 77.36 %
Mismatch	91 / 467 19.49 %	376 / 467 80.51 %

Table 4: Distribution of the paraphrase in test dataset without sentiment analysis and with polarity matching and mismatching.

3.4 Classification Algorithms

We build different models for both tasks using several widely-used classification algorithms (i.e. Decision Stump, OneR, Logistic, J48, BaysianLogisticRegression, VotedPerceptron, and MultiLayerPerceptron) to optimize 1) the Accuracy and F1-score for Paraphrase Identification and 2) the Pearson correlation of Semantic Similarity scores between system and human annotation. We use WEKA (Hall et al., 2009) to obtain robust and efficient implementation of the classifiers. We try several classification algorithms in WEKA, among others, we find that the VotedPerceptron classifier (*exponent 0.8*) returns the best result for the evaluation on training and development data. VotedPerceptron (Freund and Schapire, 1999) is a simple algorithm for linear classification which takes advantage of data that are linearly separable with large margins.

Classifier	F1-score
Baseline-1	0.502
EOP EditDistance	0.609
Decision Stump	0.736
OneR	0.733
Logistic	0.724
J48	0.721
BaysianLogisticRegression	0.723
VotedPerceptron	**0.746**
MultiLayerPerceptron	0.741

Table 5: Paraphrase Identification F1-score obtained using different classifiers on the best set of features (word/n-gram overlap + METEOR + BLEU + EditDistance).

METEOR(1)	BLEU(2)	EditDist(3)	WMF(4)	(1),(2)&(3)	(1),(2)&(4)	(2),(3)&(4)	All
0.4624	0.4022	0.4800	0.3304	**0.531**	0.471	0.515	0.526

Table 7: Semantic Similarity Results with different features on Test data.

Setup	Train&Dev	Test
Total (pairs)	18,000	972
Para	35%	32%
Non-Para	65%	68%
Selected	different trends	different times
Annotated by	5 AM Turkers	experts

Table 6: Distribution of Datasets.

4 Experiments

In this section, we describe the dataset, the task baselines and experiments carried on these two tasks.

4.1 Dataset

The dataset (Xu et al., 2014) consists of three parts, the training and development datasets (18,000 sentence pairs), the test dataset (972 sentence pairs) for evaluation. Table 6 presents the setup and distribution of all datasets used for the experiments.

Each row of data contains six tab-separated columns presenting the *Trending_Topic_Name, Sent_1, Sent_2, Label, Sent_1_tag* and *Sent_2_tag*. The *Sent_1* and *Sent_2* are two sentences which may not be necessarily full tweets. The *Label* column is in a format such like "(1, 4)", which means among 5 votes from Amazon Mechanical turkers only 1 is positive and 4 are negative. The mapping suggestions to binary labels are as follows:

- **paraphrases**: (3, 2) (4, 1) (5, 0)
- **non-paraphrases**: (1, 4) (0, 5)
- **debatable**: (2, 3) which may be discarded.

The *Sent1_tag* and *Sent2_tag* are the two sentences with part-of-speech and named entity tags. However, there is no labels of semantic similarity scores provided in development and training data, but only evaluation data.

4.2 Baselines

According to the task evaluation, we use all three baselines provided for this task which are placed at different advance levels.

Baseline-1 is a logistic regression model using simple lexical features, which is originally used in the literature (Das and Smith, 2009). It uses precision, recall and F1-score of 1-gram, 2-gram and 3-gram of tokens and stems from sentence pair to build a binary classification model for identifying paraphrase. This is the strongest baseline as it has the state-of-the-art level performance in the paraphrase identification literature.

Baseline-2 is the Weighted Matrix Factorization (WMF) model (Guo and Diab, 2012) which is a dimension reduction model to extract nuanced and robust latent vectors for short texts/sentences. To overcome the sparsity problem in short texts/sentences (e.g. 10 words on average), the missing words, a feature that LSA/LDA typically overlooks, is explicitly modeled. We use the pipeline to compute the similarity score between texts.[7]

Baseline-3 is a Random system which uses the *random* module in Python to generate a random score, in the scale [0 - 1], for each sentence pair, then it sets the threshold 0.5 for classifying *paraphrase* and *not paraphrase*.[8]

4.3 Paraphrase Identification

In order to optimize the Accuracy and F1-score for the classification, we build several models with different sets of features on the training data and evaluate these models on the development data to find the best feature set. The combination of word/n-gram, word alignment by METEOR, BLEU and EditDistance scores proves to be the most prominent set of simple features which can achieve very good performance. For classification algorithm, the VotedPerceptron returns the best result among other algorithms implemented in WEKA. In Table 1, we report the Accuracy results obtained by using different classifiers with different features. Our chosen classification algorithm and feature set outperform the strongest baseline and EOP EditDistance (standalone setting).

[7]http://www.cs.columbia.edu/%7Eweiwei/code.html

[8]https://docs.python.org/2/library/random.html

Table 5 shows F1-score obtained with different classifiers on our best set of features discovered in Table 1, and our system again results better than the strongest baseline and EOP EditDistance. Interestingly, the WMF feature which is expected to have some impact on computing the semantic similarity score does not incorporate well with other features.

4.4 Semantic Similarity

Due to no training data is given for computing the semantic similarity, a different approach is needed. Firstly, we consider to use external data from the similar task, which is Task #2 "Semantic Textual Similarity (STS)" (English STS) for training a semantic similarity model. However, after some preliminary experiments and analysis, we realize that this does not benefit our task on Twitter data due to the very big difference between formal text and informal text being used. We will need more study on how to use formal text to benefit informal text in the same task. Hence, we decide to build an unsupervised model for semantic similarity on Twitter data instead. We first adopt the result of Basline-2 (WMF) as a feature for semantic similarity. We build different unsupervised models which average the values of different sets of features learned for Paraphrase Identification task. Table 7 shows the Pearson correlation between the average of feature values and the gold similarity scores on the test data.

5 Evaluations

In this section, we discuss about the evaluation on both tasks. Table 8 shows the performance of our best models constructed by best sets of features in comparison with all the three baselines and the top three best systems reported in the shared-task.[9] For Paraphrase Identification task, our system outperforms all three baselines and achieves a very competitive result to the best systems. The difference between our system and the best three systems is a very small variance by a slim margin around 1%. In Semantic Similarity, though we only build simple model which averages the values of word alignment METEOR, BLEU and Edit Distance scores, our system still obtains better results than all three baselines and close to the top three results. These results on both tasks may place us at the 4th rank in comparison to the official ranking of the shared-task.

	PI			SS
System	Prec	Rec	F1	Pearson
Baseline-1	.679	.520	.589	.511
Baseline-2	.450	.663	.536	.350
Baseline-3	.192	.434	.266	.017
ASOBEK$^{(1^{st}\ PI)}$	.680	.669	.674	-
MITRE$^{(2^{nd}\ PI,\ 1^{st}\ SS)}$	.569	.806	.667	.619
ECNU$^{(3^{rd}\ PI)}$	.767	.583	.662	-
RTM-DCU$^{(2^{nd}\ SS)}$	-	-	-	.570
HLTC-UST$^{(3^{rd}\ SS)}$	-	-	-	.563
OurSystem	**.685**	**.634**	**.659**	**.531**

Table 8: Paraphrase Identification (PI) and Semantic Similarity (SS) Evaluation Results on Test data.

6 Error Analysis

In this section, we conduct an analysis of the misclassifications that our system makes on test data. We extract and show some randomly selected examples in which our system classifies incorrectly, both false positive or false negative; and then we analyze the possible causes for the misclassification. This inspection yields not only the top sources of error for our approach but also uncovers sources of unclear annotations in dataset.

True Positive	True Negative	False Positive	False Negative
111	612	51	64

Table 9: Error Analysis on Paraphrase Identification.

6.1 False Positive

[1357] *omg Family Guy is killing me right now - OMG we were quoting family guy*
[1357] *family guy is trending in the US - Family guy is so racist or maybe they just point out the racism in America*
[4135] *hahaha that sounds like me - That sounds totally reasonable to me*
[5211] *The world of jenks is such a real show - Jenks from the World of Jenks is such a good person*

[9]http://alt.qcri.org/semeval2015/task1/data/uploads/semeval-pit-2015-results.pdf

[128] *Anyone trying to see After Earth sometime soon - Me and my son went to see After Earth last night*

Though all these sentence pairs share many word similarity/matching and alignments, they are annotated as non-paraphrase. For example, the sentence pair **[4135]** has very high word matching and alignment after removing the common topic "sounds", but the important words "like" and "reasonable" which differ the meaning between two sentences, are not really semantically captured and distinguished by our system. As our system does not use any semantic feature, this kind of semantic difference is difficult to distinguish. Hence, it leads to false positive case.

6.2 False Negative

[4220] *Hell yeah Star Wars is on - Star Wars and lord of the rings on tv*
[785] *Chris Davis is putting the team on his back - Chris Davis doing what he does*
[400] *Rafa Benitez deserves a hell of a thank you - Any praise for Benitez from my Chelsea followers lol*
[2832] *Classy gesture by the Mets for Mariano - real class shown by The Mets Mo Rivera is a legend*
[4062] *Shonda is a freaking genius - THAT LADY IS AMAZING I LOVE SHONDA*

This case is opposite to the previous case, even though these sentence pairs do not share many word similarity and alignment, they are annotated as paraphrase. We can possibly propose some hypothesis as follows:

Extra information Though the pairs **[4220]** and **[400]** may not be paraphrase according to the paraphrase definition in the literature (Bhagat and Hovy, 2013), they are annotated as paraphrase in the gold-standard labels. In this case, we notice that as one sentence contains more extra information than the other one, it leads to low word similarity and alignment, which makes our system make wrong classification.

Specific knowledge-base In this case, the pairs **[785]** and **[2832]** require a specific knowledge-base, which is about baseball, to recognize the paraphrase; hence, even for human without any related knowledge, it might be difficult detect the paraphrase.

Common sense Though both sentences of the pair **[4062]** do not share any word similarity/alignment, they have a positive polarity that may allow identifying the paraphrase. This case may be easy for human to identify the paraphrase, yet it is difficult for machine to capture the same perception.

Table 9 shows that we can improve our system performance by exploiting more semantic features to make correct classification. Though we try to adopt the WMF which is supposed to provide more semantic information, it does not show any contribution in the overall performance. Moreover, according to our analysis for the false negative, it is rather difficult to cover these cases.

7 Conclusions and Future Work

In this paper, we study and present a set of simple features which is especially tailored to obtain very competitive performance in Paraphrase Identification and Semantic Similarity tasks on Twitter data. From the evaluation results, we can confirm our hypothesis in which the combination of word/n-grams overlap, METEOR word alignment, BLEU and Edit Distance scores can be an alternative approach to explore semantic information on Twitter data at a low cost. However, for future work, we expect to study more useful features (e.g the POS information, semantic word similarity) to improve the system performance on both identifying paraphrase and computing semantic similarity scores. From our error analysis, we consider to have more study on exploiting the semantic information for the task Semantic Similarity; and investigating on domain adaptation techniques for broad-topic data to benefit the task Paraphrase Identification in Twitter. Finally, we speculate the sentiment feature which seems to be promising in paraphrase identification task. More investigation and analysis will be needed for exploiting and integrating it with other features for better performance.

References

Rahul Bhagat and Eduard Hovy. 2013. What is a paraphrase? *Computational Linguistics*, 39(3):463–472.

Dipanjan Das and Noah A Smith. 2009. Paraphrase identification as probabilistic quasi-synchronous recognition. In *Proceedings of the Joint Conference of the 47th Annual Meeting of the ACL and the 4th International Joint Conference on Natural Language Processing of the AFNLP: Volume 1-Volume 1*, pages 468–476. Association for Computational Linguistics.

Michael Denkowski and Alon Lavie. 2014. Meteor universal: Language specific translation evaluation for any target language. In *Proceedings of the EACL 2014 Workshop on Statistical Machine Translation*.

Bill Dolan, Chris Quirk, and Chris Brockett. 2004. Unsupervised construction of large paraphrase corpora: Exploiting massively parallel news sources. In *Proceedings of the 20th international conference on Computational Linguistics*, page 350. Association for Computational Linguistics.

Samuel Fernando and Mark Stevenson. 2008. A semantic similarity approach to paraphrase detection. In *Proceedings of the 11th Annual Research Colloquium of the UK Special Interest Group for Computational Linguistics*, pages 45–52. Citeseer.

Yoav Freund and Robert E Schapire. 1999. Large margin classification using the perceptron algorithm. *Machine learning*, 37(3):277–296.

Weiwei Guo and Mona Diab. 2012. Modeling sentences in the latent space. In *Proceedings of the 50th Annual Meeting of the Association for Computational Linguistics: Long Papers-Volume 1*, pages 864–872. Association for Computational Linguistics.

Mark Hall, Eibe Frank, Geoffrey Holmes, Bernhard Pfahringer, Peter Reutemann, and Ian H Witten. 2009. The weka data mining software: an update. *ACM SIGKDD explorations newsletter*, 11(1):10–18.

Bo Han, Paul Cook, and Timothy Baldwin. 2013. Lexical normalisation of short text messages. *ACM Transactions on Intelligent Systems and Technology*, 4(1):5.

Samer Hassan and Rada Adviser-Mihalcea. 2011. *Measuring semantic relatedness using salient encyclopedic concepts*. University of North Texas.

Aminul Islam and Diana Inkpen. 2009. Semantic similarity of short texts. *Recent Advances in Natural Language Processing V*, 309:227–236.

Akshay Java, Xiaodan Song, Tim Finin, and Belle Tseng. 2007. Why we twitter: understanding microblogging usage and communities. In *Proceedings of the 9th WebKDD and 1st SNA-KDD 2007 workshop on Web mining and social network analysis*, pages 56–65. ACM.

Efthymios Kouloumpis, Theresa Wilson, and Johanna Moore. 2011. Twitter sentiment analysis: The good the bad and the omg! *ICWSM*, 11:538–541.

Balachander Krishnamurthy, Phillipa Gill, and Martin Arlitt. 2008. A few chirps about twitter. In *Proceedings of the first workshop on Online social networks*, pages 19–24. ACM.

Haewoon Kwak, Changhyun Lee, Hosung Park, and Sue Moon. 2010. What is twitter, a social network or a news media? In *Proceedings of the 19th international conference on World wide web*, pages 591–600. ACM.

Nitin Madnani and Bonnie J Dorr. 2010. Generating phrasal and sentential paraphrases: A survey of data-driven methods. *Computational Linguistics*, 36(3):341–387.

Nitin Madnani, Joel Tetreault, and Martin Chodorow. 2012. Re-examining machine translation metrics for paraphrase identification. In *Proceedings of the 2012 Conference of the North American Chapter of the Association for Computational Linguistics: Human Language Technologies*, pages 182–190. Association for Computational Linguistics.

Bernardo Magnini, Roberto Zanoli, Ido Dagan, Kathrin Eichler, Günter Neumann, Tae-Gil Noh, Sebastian Pado, Asher Stern, and Omer Levy. 2014. The excitement open platform for textual inferences.

Christopher D. Manning, Mihai Surdeanu, John Bauer, Jenny Finkel, Steven J. Bethard, and David McClosky. 2014. The Stanford CoreNLP natural language processing toolkit. In *Proceedings of 52nd Annual Meeting of the Association for Computational Linguistics: System Demonstrations*, pages 55–60.

Alexander Pak and Patrick Paroubek. 2010. Twitter as a corpus for sentiment analysis and opinion mining. In *LREC*, volume 10, pages 1320–1326.

Kishore Papineni, Salim Roukos, Todd Ward, and Wei-Jing Zhu. 2002. Bleu: a method for automatic evaluation of machine translation. In *Proceedings of the 40th annual meeting on association for computational linguistics*, pages 311–318. Association for Computational Linguistics.

Matthew G Snover, Nitin Madnani, Bonnie Dorr, and Richard Schwartz. 2009. Ter-plus: paraphrase, semantic, and alignment enhancements to translation edit rate. *Machine Translation*, 23(2-3):117–127.

Richard Socher, Eric H Huang, Jeffrey Pennin, Christopher D Manning, and Andrew Y Ng. 2011. Dynamic pooling and unfolding recursive autoencoders for paraphrase detection. In *Advances in Neural Information Processing Systems*, pages 801–809.

Stephen Wan, Mark Dras, Robert Dale, and Cécile Paris. 2006. Using dependency-based features to take the "para-farce" out of paraphrase. In *Proceedings of the Australasian Language Technology Workshop*, volume 2006.

Wei Xu, Alan Ritter, and Ralph Grishman. 2013. Gathering and generating paraphrases from twitter with application to normalization. In *Proceedings of the Sixth Workshop on Building and Using Comparable Corpora*, pages 121–128. Citeseer.

Wei Xu, Alan Ritter, Chris Callison-Burch, William B Dolan, and Yangfeng Ji. 2014. Extracting lexically divergent paraphrases from twitter. *Transactions Of The Association For Computational Linguistics*, 2:435–448.

Wei Xu, Chris Callison-Burch, and William B. Dolan. 2015. SemEval-2015 Task 1: Paraphrase and semantic similarity in Twitter (PIT). In *Proceedings of the*

9th International Workshop on Semantic Evaluation (SemEval).

Fabio Massimo Zanzotto, Marco Pennacchiotti, and Kostas Tsioutsiouliklis. 2011. Linguistic redundancy in twitter. In *Proceedings of the Conference on Empirical Methods in Natural Language Processing*, pages 659–669. Association for Computational Linguistics.

A Language Detection System for Short Chats in Mobile Games

Pidong Wang **Nikhil Bojja** **Shivasankari Kannan**

Machine Zone Inc.
2225 East Bayshore Road, Suite 200
Palo Alto, CA 94303, USA

{pwang,nbojja,skannan}@machinezone.com

Abstract

Machine Translation system accuracies are often brought down due to inaccurate Language Detection (LD) of input phrases. The Language detection accuracy is further affected when the inputs are short and contain ungrammatical phrases, especially in a multilingual mobile game setting. Chat messages in mobile games are often short as they are typed on mobile devices and contain slang as a common communication preference. Previous work has shown that LD systems have a drop in accuracy when the inputs are short messages instead of long ones. This paper targets LD for short chat messages in mobile games. We propose a novel LD system which integrates text-based and user-based methods to achieve significantly better performance over current state-of-the-art LD systems.

1 Introduction

With the growth of social media, a huge amount of social media texts have become ubiquitous, e.g., Twitter messages, Facebook updates, game chat messages, etc. Due to their importance, Natural Language Processing (NLP) applications have been applied to social media texts, e.g., Liu et al. (2011) and Ritter et al. (2011) recognized named entities in Twitter messages, and Foster et al. (2011) investigated Part-Of-Speech tagging and parsing of Twitter messages. As the phenomenon is prevelant across the globe, social media texts are usually multilingual, while most of the NLP applications are language-specific. We usually have to know the language of a given message, in order to process the message using appropriate NLP applications. Accuracy of Language Detection (LD) is thus highly critical for subsequent NLP applications.

LD on long messages is widely considered a solved problem as its accuracy is often found to be high with latest methods (Ahmed et al., 2004; Hughes et al., 2006; Grothe et al., 2008). However, more and more researchers have recently noted that LD on short messages is very difficult. E.g, Baldwin and Lui (2010) found LD became increasingly difficult as we reduced the length of documents, and increased the number of languages. Carter et al. (2013) found LD of microblogs was challenging for state-of-the-art LD methods. Moreover, LD studies mostly focus on Twitter messages, as Twitter provides an API for researchers to crawl public Twitter messages, while no research is done on game chat messages, which in itself contains language that has quite a bit more slang than Twitter messages.

In this paper, we propose a novel LD system for chat messages in a mobile game which has a built-in chat translation system. The translation system helps players speaking different languages chat with each other. The LD system is used to detect language of chat messages such that the chat translation system could know which language a message should be translated from. Chat messages in mobile games are different from other social media texts, because it is inconvenient to type on mobile devices leading to an increased misspelling rate, and game chats tend to be much shorter than Twitter messages (see Section 3). Our work is further more challenging, as we are detecting 27 languages.

Our contributions are as follows: (a) as far as we

Proceedings of SocialNLP 2015@NAACL-HLT, pages 20–28,
Denver, Colorado, June 5, 2015.

know, this work is the first LD work on game chat messages, so our work may pave the way to NLP research on game chat messages which are a new kind of social media texts; (b) our work is also the first approach to apply user language profiles to the LD of game chat messages; (c) we have shown that LD of game chats is very difficult and also propose a novel LD system integrating both text-based and user-based methods to achieve significantly better performance over the current state-of-the-art LD systems.

2 Related Work

Language Detection (LD), or Language Identification (LI), has been extensively studied in previous work. One famous method is character n-gram-based approach (Cavnar and Trenkle, 1994) which was based on calculating and comparing profiles of n-gram frequencies via "Out Of Place" (OOP) distance, a ranking-based distance. The approach first computed a profile for each language in a multilingual training set. Given a test document, the approach computed a profile that was then compared to each language profile obtained from the training set. The document was detected as a language which had the smallest distance to the document's profile. This approach achieved a 99.8% accuracy on Usenet newsgroup articles. One of the disadvantages of (Cavnar and Trenkle, 1994) is that it requires the input to be tokenized. Another similar approach was done by Dunning (1994) who used byte n-grams instead of character n-grams, avoiding the tokenization problem. This approach achieved 99.9% accuracy on documents longer than 500 bytes.

Recently, many researchers have noticed the difficulty in LD for short documents/messages. For example, Baldwin and Lui (2010) presented a detailed investigation of what approaches were the best in varied conditions, and found that LD became more and more difficult when we increased the number of languages, reduced the size of training data and reduced the length of documents. Vatanen et al. (2010) investigated a LD task where the test samples had only 5-21 characters. The authors compared two approaches: one was a naive Bayes classifier based on character n-gram models, and the other was the OOP method of Cavnar and Trenkle (1994). To improve LD on short and ill-written texts, Tromp and Pechenizkiy (2011) proposed a graph-based n-gram approach (LIGA) which performed better than the character n-gram approach of Cavnar and Trenkle (1994) on Twitter messages. Based on LIGA, Vogel and Tresner-Kirsch (2012) further proposed some linguitistically-motivated changes to LIGA, achieving an accuracy of 99.8% on Twitter messages in 6 European languages, while the accuracy of LIGA was 97.9% on the same test set. Bergsma et al. (2012) focused on LD on short, informal texts in resource-poor languages, annotating and releasing a large collection of Twitter messages in 9 languages using 3 scripts: Cyrillic, Arabic and Devanagari. The authors also presented two LD systems which achieved very high accuracy on Twitter messages.

All the previous work focused on LD using text features. In contrast, our work utilizes user language profile as well, i.e., language distribution of messages sent by a user, to further improve LD on very short messages. The most relevant work was done by Carter et al. (2013). In order to improve LD of Twitter messages, the authors used post-dependent features (i.e., features from only texts) together with several post-independent features: the language profile of a blogger, the content of an attached hyperlink, the language profile of a tag, and the language of the original post. However, we could not directly apply their approach to our context, chat messages in games which are different from Twitter messages, e.g., chat messages have no hyperlink, no tag, etc. Furthermore, game chats are often much shorter than Twitter messages, so LD of game chats is much more challenging (Section 3).

Another relevant line of research is on LD for search engine queries in the context of Cross Language Information Retrieval (CLIR), as the queries are usually relatively short like game chats. Ceylan and Kim (2009) first generated a LD data set of search engine queries extracted from click-through logs of Yahoo! Search Engine, and then trained decision tree classifiers for LD. Moreover, the authors also experimented with a non-text feature, the language information of the country from which a user makes a search query. Gottron and Lipka (2010) used news headlines as short, query-style texts on which several typical LD approaches had been evaluated. In their experiments, the naive Bayes classifier with character n-gram features performed best among others. Nevertheless, search engine queries are different from our focus, game chats, in the sense that search queries are usually well-written words/phrases, while game chats could be ill-written, short phrases/sentences.

3 Chat Messages of Mobile Games

To better understand the differences between game chat messages and Twitter messages, we have crawled 2,308,264 Twitter messages using a Java implementation[1] of Twitter's stream API[2]. On average, each message has 73.51 characters. On the other hand, we have obtained 745,635,448 game chat messages from a chat log database of a Massively Multiplayer Online Role Playing mobile Game (MMORPG). Each game chat message has 34.43 characters on average.

From these statistics, we could see that game chat messages are about two times shorter than Twitter messages, despite the different language distributions of the two message sets.

4 Methods

In this section, we will first describe how we make a multilingual data set for LD based on a chat log database of a mobile game. We then present a novel approach to LD for game chat messages. Generally, our approach has two steps: the first step uses an alphabet-based LD method, and the second step uses a linear model (Fan et al., 2008) to integrate 3 methods together: a byte n-gram-based method (Lui and Baldwin, 2012), a dictionary-based method, and a method based on user language profiles. The alphabet-based LD method will be introduced, followed by the 3 methods. We then present our approach by explaining how we integrate the 4 methods together.

4.1 Game Chat Data Collection

In this subsection, we will describe how we make a multilingual data set of game chat messages, based on a chat log database of a mobile game. All the data are encoded in UTF-8.

Generally, a chat log database of a mobile game is accessible. The database contains many fields for a message. Among the fields, related ones to our work are the string of a message, a unique identifier for each user (user id) for the message sender, and the language of the last keyboard used to enter the message. What we want to make is a data set containing many chat messages, for each of which we need its true language and user id.

An important question to answer at this stage is whether we could rely on the keyboard language to find the true language for a message. The answer is no. There are two main reasons for this. The first one is that users might use a keyboard to input a message in a language which is different from the language of the keyboard, e.g., a French user might use English keyboard to input a French message to avoid the delay caused by changing keyboards. The other reason is that users tend to use special keyboards on mobile devices, e.g., a user could input an English message with an English keyboard and then an Emoji[3] with an Emoji keyboard, in which case the log database only records the last keyboard, i.e., the Emoji keyboard.

Motivated by Ceylan and Kim (2009) who generated a LD data set of search engine queries extracted from click-through logs of Yahoo! Search Engine, we could also use the chat log database to make a LD data set. More specifically, we first sample our chat log database to get a raw data set containing messages written using different keyboards according to the keyboard language field. For each message in the raw data set, the LD API of the Microsoft Translator[4] is used to detect the language of the message. If the detected language matches the keyboard language field, we consider the message as a valid message in the final LD data set.

4.2 ALPHA: Alphabet-Based LD

The most straight-forward way to do LD is to count the number of characters of each language, given a message, then picking the language with the highest number of characters. We call this method alphabet-based language detection whose algorithm is shown in Algorithm 1. We use a third-party library which

[1] `http://twitter4j.org/en/code-examples.html#streaming`

[2] `https://dev.twitter.com/streaming/overview`

[3] `http://en.wikipedia.org/wiki/Emoji`

[4] `http://msdn.microsoft.com/en-us/library/ff512411.aspx`

could return all the characters used by a given language.

Algorithm 1 Alphabet-Based Language Detection

```
INPUT: a raw message M whose length is N
RETURN: the detected language for M
initialize a map char2langList which maps a character to a list of languages;
initialize a map lang2count which maps a language to the count of characters of the language in M;
for i ← 0 to N-1 do
    for each lang in char2langList[M[i]] do
        lang2count[lang] ← lang2count[lang] + 1;
return the language in lang2count with the highest count;
```

This method is effective when distinguishing languages written in different scripts, e.g., Chinese and English. However, it is not good at distinguishing languages using similar scripts, e.g., languages using the Latin script. Thus, to achieve a good performance, this method should be used together with other methods, e.g., we could use this method to detect languages using almost separate scripts, e.g., Thai, Chinese, Japanese, Korean, etc. and then use other methods to detect other languages. Please note that here "almost separate scripts" depends on the target language set we want to detect, e.g., if the set contains Russian and Ukrainian both of which use the Cyrillic script, we'd better not use the alphabet-based LD method to detect Russian or Ukrainian, while if the set only contains Russian without Ukrainian, we could detect Russian with the method.

Another issue with this method is the situation that multiple languages have the same highest count. Our solution is to set a priority list of languages according to the language frequencies in the game and language-specific knowledge, and we choose the first language in the list with the highest count of characters as the detected language.

4.3 LANGID: Byte N-Gram-Based LD

Our LD system uses a byte n-gram-based LD approach (Lui and Baldwin, 2012). This approach essentially uses a naive Bayes classifier with byte n-gram features.

Lui and Baldwin (2012) have released an off-the-shelf LD tool written in Python as an implementation of the approach. We have rewritten the tool in C++ to get a higher processing speed. A pre-trained model is released with the tool, and was trained on a large amount of multilingual texts from various domains (Lui and Baldwin, 2011) in 97 languages. The tool also provides a way to limit the number of languages to a subset of the 97 languages, to achieve a higher accuracy and speed. Given an input, the tool has an API to normalize confidence scores for each language to probability values.

4.4 DICT: Dictionary-Based LD

Assuming words in an input message are space-delimited, we could count the number of words in each language, then picking the language with the highest number of words as the detected language. We call this method dictionary-based language detection whose algorithm is shown in Algorithm 2.

Algorithm 2 Dictionary-Based Language Detection

```
INPUT: a raw message M
RETURN: the detected language for M
tokenize M into a sequence of words WORDS whose length is N, ignoring punctuation;
initialize a map word2langList which maps a word to a list of languages;
initialize a map lang2count which maps a language to the count of words of the language in WORDS;
for i ← 0 to N-1 do
    for each lang in word2langList[WORDS[i]] do
        lang2count[lang] ← lang2count[lang] + 1;
return the language in lang2count with the highest count;
```

The advantage of this method is that it works well on short messages, even if the input message is only one word, while its disadvantage is from its assumption, i.e., the words of the input message should be space-delimited, which limits the applicability of this method. For example, without knowing an input message is Chinese, the input message cannot be tokenized into words properly, while knowing the language of the input message is just the job of LD. Furthermore, as we are dealing with game chat messages, users could use informal words, e.g., "u" instead of "you", "gtg" instead of "got to go", etc. which also pose difficulties for the dictionaries used in this method. To overcome this problem, e.g., we could use methods like (Liu et al., 2012) to extend our dictionaries to include informal words and slang terms. Another issue with the method is that multiple languages could have the same word, e.g., for a message containing only one word which occurs in two languages, we could also set a language priority list to solve this problem as in Section 4.2.

4.5 PROFILE: User Language Profile

As can be seen from Section 3, game chat messages are often very short. LD methods relying on only text-based features would perform poorly on game chats. In this subsection, we will introduce a novel method to LD of game chat messages: user language profiles. A language profile for a user is a vector of real numbers each of which represents the probability of sending a message in a particular language. The size of the vector is the same for all the users, i.e., the number of languages supported by the game, though most users only speak one or two languages. In order to build the language profiles, ideally, we should have many human annotators to annotate all the chat messages sent in the game, but it is impractical. We thus have to choose an automatic LD system to detect the language of each message sent by a user. As a result, we obtain a vector of the count of messages written in each language. We then normalize the counts into probabilities, getting a vector of probabilities as the language profile for the user. The LANGID system (Section 4.3) is used here to build language profiles. Of course, the LD system might make errors, especially on short messages. However, the experimental results (Section 5.3) confirm this way of building language profiles is effective.

For a new user, the probabilities in the language profile are all 0, meaning we do not know what language the new user will use. If we use PROFILE individually, the first language in its language priority list is chosen.

4.6 COMB: Combined System

In this subsection, we will show how we integrate all the methods mentioned in this section together to make a high-performance LD system for chat messages sent in mobile games.

Work Flow: According to the characteristics of the methods mentioned in this section, our system has two phases: Phase 1 uses the ALPHA LD (Section 4.2) to detect languages using "separate" scripts; Phase 2 uses a linear model to combine the byte n-gram-based method (Section 4.3), the dictionary-based method (Section 4.4) and the user language profile (Section 4.5) together to detect the rest of languages in the target language set. The work flow of the combined LD system is presented in Figure 1.

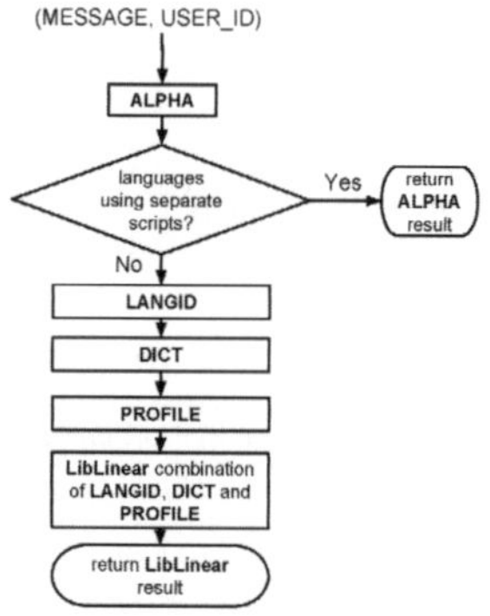

Figure 1: Work flow of the combined LD system.

LibLinear: A linear model is used to combine the three methods which are respectively presented in Section 4.3, 4.4, and 4.5. More precisely, we use the linear support vector machines in LibLinear (Fan et al., 2008) as the linear model. LibLinear is an open source library which is very efficient for large-scale linear classification. We have also tried the SVM model with linear kernel in LibSVM (Chang and Lin, 2011) instead of LibLinear, but LibSVM is much slower than LibLinear with similar accuracies. We thus choose LibLinear finally.

E.g., if the game language set is {Chinese, English, French, Thai}, in Phase 1, the ALPHA method detects the 4 languages. If the result is in {Chinese, Thai}, we stop and return the result. Otherwise, English and French are detected in Phase 2. The input feature vector of LibLinear is a concatenation of the normalized output vectors from LANGID, DICT, and PROFILE. Each of the output vectors has 2 real numbers indicating the probability of being English or French. The output vector of DICT may be shorter than that of the other two, when DICT is not applicable to some languages, e.g., a lack of dictionaries, or words which are not space-delimited.

5 Experiments

5.1 Evaluation Corpora

As far as we know, most previous LD work on short messages (Tromp and Pechenizkiy, 2011; Vogel and Tresner-Kirsch, 2012) focused on Twitter messages, and no previous work explored LD for game chat messages. We thus create a LD data set containing multilingual chat messages sent in mobile games with the method described in Section 4.1.

We first create a data set containing chat messages

Languages	Data set statistics (#lines / #characters)					
	TRAIN	**LEN1**	**LEN2**	**LEN3**	**LEN4**	**FULL**
Arabic	17153 / 444779	634 / 2834	984 / 8845	1000 / 13164	1000 / 16667	1000 / 25796
Catalan	8585 / 207730	452 / 2096	838 / 6968	918 / 11196	980 / 16143	1000 / 24190
Chinese	10705 / 110612	695 / 1379	992 / 3784	1000 / 5334	1000 / 6526	1000 / 10620
Czech	7612 / 259388	645 / 3059	965 / 8544	998 / 13336	1000 / 17347	1000 / 33426
Danish	11031 / 554513	367 / 1690	804 / 6992	969 / 12619	996 / 17397	1000 / 50660
Dutch	1201 / 52307	457 / 2206	891 / 8027	985 / 13576	997 / 18768	1000 / 44200
English	68035 / 3134196	473 / 2171	876 / 7736	985 / 13471	998 / 18692	1000 / 46310
Finnish	4003 / 151253	631 / 3286	949 / 9713	981 / 15171	996 / 20196	1000 / 36283
French	27555 / 1197251	416 / 1875	853 / 7024	982 / 12233	998 / 17021	1000 / 43362
German	10978 / 448484	509 / 2441	950 / 8681	997 / 14052	999 / 19214	1000 / 41333
Greek	18234 / 801094	517 / 2845	956 / 9498	999 / 14454	1000 / 18665	1000 / 43668
Hebrew	18553 / 512033	492 / 2115	911 / 7614	996 / 12363	1000 / 15945	1000 / 28842
Hungarian	6876 / 236017	634 / 3285	965 / 9503	997 / 14357	1000 / 18590	1000 / 32241
Indonesian	10285 / 380596	664 / 3309	987 / 9548	1000 / 14902	1000 / 19735	1000 / 35899
Italian	5528 / 256781	539 / 2790	958 / 9066	996 / 14509	998 / 19801	1000 / 46734
Japanese	12531 / 249595	718 / 1414	923 / 3563	976 / 5407	988 / 6938	1000 / 19193
Korean	16546 / 285583	615 / 1180	948 / 3518	986 / 5446	999 / 7152	1000 / 17464
Malay	8899 / 277092	643 / 3075	968 / 9039	993 / 14171	999 / 19154	1000 / 30792
Norwegian	7308 / 316033	419 / 1947	812 / 7031	964 / 12601	997 / 17406	1000 / 43412
Polish	382 / 16481	312 / 1563	483 / 4650	495 / 7587	496 / 10303	500 / 21699
Portuguese	10493 / 414901	549 / 2827	944 / 8794	994 / 14449	1000 / 19554	1000 / 39585
Romanian	9823 / 301461	543 / 2502	929 / 7969	990 / 12894	1000 / 17072	1000 / 30832
Russian	14060 / 592906	484 / 2589	833 / 7866	977 / 14091	998 / 19734	1000 / 41726
Slovak	7482 / 320377	551 / 2757	929 / 8313	994 / 13625	1000 / 18670	1000 / 41426
Spanish	4785 / 237427	477 / 2503	915 / 8322	992 / 13829	998 / 18995	1000 / 49421
Swedish	9044 / 410050	462 / 2243	888 / 7875	987 / 13247	1000 / 17760	1000 / 44829
Turkish	614 / 29611	615 / 3372	976 / 10771	1000 / 17285	1000 / 23733	1000 / 49008

Table 1: Statistics of the LD data sets created from game chat messages.

in 27 languages supported by the game, then splitting the messages for each language into a training set (named **TRAIN**) and a test set (named **FULL**). As our focus is on short messages, we also generate four other test sets based on **FULL**. We have truncated each message in **FULL** to retain the first n tokens[5], thus generating 4 new test sets named as **LEN**n where $n \in \{1, 2, 3, 4\}$. In **LEN**n, only unique messages are retained based on only texts, e.g., if we have (text="thx tom", userid="123", lang="en") and (text="thx boss", userid="456", lang="en") in **FULL**, we only keep one message (text="thx", userid="123", lang="en") generated from the two messages in the data set **LEN1**. The statistics of the resulted data sets are shown in Table 1.

Following Carter et al. (2013), we also use accuracy, i.e., the percentage of messages whose language is detected correctly, to evaluate the effect of LD.

5.2 Systems

We compare our proposed LD system (COMB of Section 4.6) against three baseline methods:
(1) LANGID: uses the byte n-gram-based LD method described in Section 4.3 with the 27 languages of Table 1; we have tried to train a new model with the data **TRAIN** in Table 1, but the new model works worse than the pre-trained model, which may be due to the fact that the amount of **TRAIN** is much smaller than that used to train the pre-trained model; the pre-trained model is thus used in our experiments; this system has already been shown superior to many methods, e.g., TextCat which is an implementation of (Cavnar and Trenkle, 1994) and CLD which is the embedded LD system used in Google's Chromium Browser, so we do not compare our COMB to these methods in this paper;
(2) DICT: uses the dictionary-based LD method described in Section 4.4 to detect 10 languages[6], as we only have dictionaries for the 10 languages;
(3) PROFILE: the user language profile method described in Section 4.5; the user language profiles of the 27 languages have been built using LANGID;

The COMB system uses the alphabet-based LD method (Section 4.2) to detect the 27 languages in Phase 1. If the result is in {Arabic, Hebrew, Greek, Russian, Chinese, Japanese, Korean}, we stop and

[5] if words are not space-delimited in a language, the first $2 \times n$ characters are kept

[6] the priority language list is {English, French, Spanish, German, Portuguese, Russian, Dutch, Polish, Italian, Turkish}

return the result. Otherwise, in Phase 2, COMB uses LibLinear (Section 4.6) to combine LANGID, DICT and PROFILE together to detect the 20 languages, which are the 27 languages of Table 1 minus the 7 languages detected by Phase 1. The LibLinear model is trained on the data **TRAIN** of Table 1.

5.3 Experimental Results

The experimental results on data set **LEN1** are shown in Table 2, from which we can see that for extremely short messages containing only 1 token, LANGID performs poorly with an average accuracy of 34.88%. DICT works better than LANGID on the 10 languages supported by DICT, which shows that dictionary-based methods are very useful in LD for short messages, though detecting 10 languages is much easier than detecting 27 languages. Moreover, PROFILE achieves very amazing accuracies on 1-token messages, which confirms the critical importance of user language profiles in LD of very short messages. At last, COMB successfully combines the three systems above and the alphabet-based LD method, achieving a relatively high accuracy of 73.69% on 1-token messages, which outperforms PROFILE by 11.48% accuracy. Note that the **AVERAGE** is macro-average.

Table 3, 4 and 5 respectively present the results on data set **LEN2**, **LEN3** and **LEN4**. LANGID's accuracy increases as the message length increases, as expected. Because more text is available. PROFILE maintains a stable accuracy at about 63.5% on all the 3 data sets, since it only depends on the user who sends the message, and is independent on texts. COMB again performs best among the 4 systems.

The experimental results on data set **FULL** are shown in Table 6. LANGID works much better on full-length messages than on shorter messages. PROFILE still keeps a stable accuracy at 63.57%. COMB performs best with an average accuracy of 84.61% on the 27 languages.

As a summary, the average accuracy of LANGID varies from 34.88% to 74.53% on the 5 test sets of messages of different lengths, which shows that the traditional LD methods relying on text-based features perform poorly on short messages. PROFILE works consistently well on the test sets with an accuracy at about 63%. Our proposed system COMB can effectively integrate LANGID, DICT, and PROFILE

Languages	LANGID	DICT	PROFILE	COMB
Arabic	96.85	N.A.	86.75	97.16
Catalan	1.55	N.A.	9.29	42.04
Chinese	94.96	N.A.	80.29	98.56
Czech	14.57	N.A.	47.75	62.33
Danish	14.44	N.A.	74.66	86.92
Dutch	8.10	25.60	53.17	70.46
English	89.43	100.00	99.79	94.08
Finnish	22.50	N.A.	42.16	57.05
French	13.22	29.09	93.51	82.69
German	24.36	35.76	91.55	93.52
Greek	90.33	N.A.	66.34	90.91
Hebrew	85.57	N.A.	84.76	92.48
Hungarian	20.03	N.A.	52.21	58.36
Indonesian	6.02	N.A.	23.04	82.23
Italian	9.09	32.28	89.98	92.58
Japanese	65.60	N.A.	40.53	65.18
Korean	85.04	N.A.	68.46	88.94
Malay	0.16	N.A.	0.00	14.62
Norwegian	2.39	N.A.	33.65	61.58
Polish	23.72	41.99	32.69	56.09
Portuguese	5.28	42.81	88.89	96.36
Romanian	7.37	N.A.	30.57	62.62
Russian	79.75	82.44	98.55	86.16
Slovak	8.53	N.A.	40.47	73.50
Spanish	22.64	42.14	93.71	43.40
Swedish	18.40	N.A.	67.53	87.45
Turkish	31.87	42.11	89.43	52.36
Average	34.88	N.A.	62.21	73.69

Table 2: Accuracies (%) of LD methods on **LEN1**.

Languages	LANGID	DICT	PROFILE	COMB
Arabic	99.80	N.A.	86.69	99.80
Catalan	1.79	N.A.	7.52	43.56
Chinese	95.46	N.A.	81.15	99.40
Czech	24.97	N.A.	50.88	70.98
Danish	33.96	N.A.	74.50	90.80
Dutch	25.48	31.43	54.10	70.15
English	77.40	100.00	99.66	92.58
Finnish	44.47	N.A.	43.84	62.91
French	37.16	33.06	94.37	85.23
German	43.47	46.32	91.89	92.53
Greek	98.43	N.A.	71.23	98.64
Hebrew	96.71	N.A.	86.17	99.67
Hungarian	37.20	N.A.	56.37	65.08
Indonesian	22.90	N.A.	21.99	85.31
Italian	32.25	46.03	91.86	94.05
Japanese	84.40	N.A.	41.93	83.42
Korean	91.56	N.A.	71.52	93.99
Malay	3.31	N.A.	0.00	14.88
Norwegian	16.87	N.A.	35.34	64.29
Polish	37.06	54.66	33.75	54.24
Portuguese	17.37	51.80	91.00	96.82
Romanian	12.59	N.A.	34.02	70.61
Russian	96.64	94.72	98.80	97.84
Slovak	14.10	N.A.	41.66	76.43
Spanish	50.38	52.02	94.54	46.89
Swedish	38.96	N.A.	68.69	91.55
Turkish	52.46	63.22	89.45	62.50
Average	47.67	N.A.	63.44	77.93

Table 3: Accuracies (%) of LD methods on **LEN2**.

Languages	LANGID	DICT	PROFILE	COMB
Arabic	99.90	N.A.	86.90	99.90
Catalan	8.17	N.A.	7.08	42.48
Chinese	96.60	N.A.	81.10	99.50
Czech	36.27	N.A.	50.60	72.34
Danish	48.30	N.A.	75.44	92.98
Dutch	40.61	46.60	54.31	74.31
English	70.76	100.00	99.70	91.17
Finnish	55.76	N.A.	43.02	66.26
French	51.12	40.02	94.91	88.19
German	59.18	63.59	91.98	94.08
Greek	99.50	N.A.	71.27	99.70
Hebrew	99.60	N.A.	86.25	99.90
Hungarian	44.93	N.A.	56.17	65.20
Indonesian	33.90	N.A.	22.30	87.70
Italian	54.12	64.96	92.07	95.18
Japanese	88.32	N.A.	42.62	88.32
Korean	93.71	N.A.	71.40	96.04
Malay	6.55	N.A.	0.00	13.90
Norwegian	34.02	N.A.	36.41	65.66
Polish	52.93	66.26	33.74	58.38
Portuguese	33.80	67.40	90.74	96.68
Romanian	23.13	N.A.	34.44	71.92
Russian	99.59	98.67	98.77	99.59
Slovak	23.74	N.A.	42.25	77.87
Spanish	62.20	69.66	94.96	61.09
Swedish	53.90	N.A.	68.69	93.52
Turkish	71.10	76.70	89.50	76.90
Average	57.10	N.A.	63.58	80.32

Table 4: Accuracies (%) of LD methods on **LEN3**.

Languages	LANGID	DICT	PROFILE	COMB
Arabic	99.90	N.A.	86.90	99.90
Catalan	15.31	N.A.	6.63	44.39
Chinese	97.00	N.A.	81.10	99.60
Czech	42.30	N.A.	50.60	72.30
Danish	54.12	N.A.	75.90	93.78
Dutch	53.66	59.48	54.56	76.83
English	75.75	100.00	99.70	92.89
Finnish	59.64	N.A.	42.37	66.57
French	65.93	51.80	94.99	92.18
German	69.07	73.67	91.99	95.20
Greek	99.50	N.A.	71.30	99.70
Hebrew	99.60	N.A.	86.30	99.90
Hungarian	50.40	N.A.	56.00	65.90
Indonesian	44.20	N.A.	22.30	88.80
Italian	69.14	77.25	92.08	95.49
Japanese	91.30	N.A.	43.22	91.70
Korean	95.60	N.A.	71.47	97.60
Malay	11.21	N.A.	0.00	13.31
Norwegian	48.95	N.A.	36.51	67.10
Polish	56.65	73.19	33.67	62.10
Portuguese	46.60	78.30	90.80	97.00
Romanian	29.20	N.A.	34.60	72.00
Russian	100.00	99.80	98.80	100.00
Slovak	30.10	N.A.	42.10	78.40
Spanish	73.15	81.76	94.89	72.65
Swedish	63.40	N.A.	68.90	94.20
Turkish	82.40	84.00	89.50	85.50
Average	63.85	N.A.	63.60	82.04

Table 5: Accuracies (%) of LD methods on **LEN4**.

Languages	LANGID	DICT	PROFILE	COMB
Arabic	99.90	N.A.	86.90	99.90
Catalan	22.50	N.A.	6.50	44.80
Chinese	97.10	N.A.	81.10	99.80
Czech	51.20	N.A.	50.60	72.40
Danish	61.80	N.A.	75.90	95.00
Dutch	80.70	86.70	54.50	80.80
English	90.60	100.00	99.70	96.80
Finnish	62.30	N.A.	42.20	66.80
French	88.60	83.80	95.00	96.10
German	85.00	90.10	92.00	96.30
Greek	99.60	N.A.	71.30	99.80
Hebrew	99.70	N.A.	86.30	100.00
Hungarian	54.80	N.A.	56.00	66.30
Indonesian	52.80	N.A.	22.30	89.80
Italian	91.10	95.10	92.10	96.10
Japanese	95.80	N.A.	43.10	97.70
Korean	97.90	N.A.	71.50	100.00
Malay	16.50	N.A.	0.00	12.10
Norwegian	67.50	N.A.	36.50	70.10
Polish	70.60	81.40	33.40	70.20
Portuguese	71.20	94.30	90.80	97.30
Romanian	42.60	N.A.	34.60	72.70
Russian	100.00	100.00	98.80	100.00
Slovak	47.40	N.A.	42.10	78.80
Spanish	94.40	99.00	94.90	95.00
Swedish	76.90	N.A.	68.90	94.50
Turkish	93.90	94.20	89.50	95.30
Average	74.53	N.A.	63.57	84.61

Table 6: Accuracies (%) of LD methods on **FULL**.

together, consistently outperforming all the baselines on test sets of messages of different lengths. COMB achieves a relatively consistent and high accuracy on messages of varied lengths from 73.69% to 84.61%. These results confirm the potential of the proposed system.

We also found both LANGID and COMB perform poorly on Malay and Catalan, which may be due to the fact that Malay is very similar to Indonesian, and that Catalan is similar to French and Spanish.

6 Conclusion

This paper presents a novel LD system for chat messages in mobile games. The system can effectively integrate both text-based and user-based LD methods. In our experiments, we achieve highly statistically significant ($p < 0.0001$ in T-test) improvements (10.08%-18.19% in absolute accuracy) over strong baselines on 27-language test sets which contain messages of various lengths.

Future work can investigate how to preprocess or normalize game chat messages to further improve LD. Moreover, adding more dictionaries may also be a future direction to improve the accuracy of the proposed LD system.

References

Bashir Ahmed, Sung-Hyuk Cha, and Charles Tappert. 2004. Language identification from text using n-gram based cumulative frequency addition. In *Proceedings of Student/Faculty Research Day, CSIS, Pace University*.

Timothy Baldwin and Marco Lui. 2010. Language identification: The long and the short of the matter. In *Proceedings of NAACL-HLT*.

Shane Bergsma, Paul McNamee, Mossaab Bagdouri, Clayton Fink, and Theresa Wilson. 2012. Language identification for creating language-specific Twitter collections. In *Proceedings of the Second Workshop on Language in Social Media*.

Simon Carter, Wouter Weerkamp, and Manos Tsagkias. 2013. Microblog language identification: Overcoming the limitations of short, unedited and idiomatic text. *Language Resources and Evaluation*, 47(1):195–215.

William B. Cavnar and John M. Trenkle. 1994. N-gram-based text categorization. In *Proceedings of the Third Symposium on Document Analysis and Information Retrieval*.

Hakan Ceylan and Yookyung Kim. 2009. Language identification of search engine queries. In *Proceedings of ACL-IJCNLP*.

Chih-Chung Chang and Chih-Jen Lin. 2011. LIBSVM: A library for support vector machines. *ACM Transactions on Intelligent Systems and Technology*, 2:27:1–27:27. Software available at `http://www.csie.ntu.edu.tw/~cjlin/libsvm`.

Ted Dunning. 1994. *Statistical identification of language*. Computing Research Laboratory, New Mexico State University.

Rong-En Fan, Kai-Wei Chang, Cho-Jui Hsieh, Xiang-Rui Wang, and Chih-Jen Lin. 2008. LIBLINEAR: A library for large linear classification. *Journal of Machine Learning Research*, 9:1871–1874.

Jennifer Foster, Özlem Çetinoglu, Joachim Wagner, Joseph Le Roux, Stephen Hogan, Joakim Nivre, Deirdre Hogan, and Josef Van Genabith. 2011. # hardtoparse: POS tagging and parsing the twitterverse. In *Proceedings of the AAAI Workshop On Analyzing Microtext*.

Thomas Gottron and Nedim Lipka. 2010. A comparison of language identification approaches on short, query-style texts. In *Advances in information retrieval*, pages 611–614. Springer.

Lena Grothe, Ernesto William De Luca, and Andreas Nürnberger. 2008. A comparative study on language identification methods. In *Proceedings of LREC*.

Baden Hughes, Timothy Baldwin, Steven Bird, Jeremy Nicholson, and Andrew MacKinlay. 2006. Reconsidering language identification for written language resources. In *Proceedings of LREC*.

Xiaohua Liu, Shaodian Zhang, Furu Wei, and Ming Zhou. 2011. Recognizing named entities in tweets. In *Proceedings of ACL-HLT*.

Fei Liu, Fuliang Weng, and Xiao Jiang. 2012. A broad-coverage normalization system for social media language. In *Proceedings of ACL*.

Marco Lui and Timothy Baldwin. 2011. Cross-domain feature selection for language identification. In *In Proceedings of IJCNLP*.

Marco Lui and Timothy Baldwin. 2012. langid.py: An off-the-shelf language identification tool. In *Proceedings of ACL System Demonstrations*.

Alan Ritter, Sam Clark, Mausam, and Oren Etzioni. 2011. Named entity recognition in tweets: An experimental study. In *Proceedings of EMNLP*.

Erik Tromp and Mykola Pechenizkiy. 2011. Graph-based n-gram language identification on short texts. In *Proceedings of the 20th Machine Learning conference of Belgium and The Netherlands*.

Tommi Vatanen, Jaakko J. Väyrynen, and Sami Virpioja. 2010. Language identification of short text segments with n-gram models. In *Proceedings of LREC*.

John Vogel and David Tresner-Kirsch. 2012. Robust language identification in short, noisy texts: Improvements to LIGA. In *Proceedings of The Third International Workshop on Mining Ubiquitous and Social Environments*.

Long Nights, Rainy Days, and Misspent Youth: Automatically Extracting and Categorizing Occasions Associated with Consumer Products

David B. Bracewell
Oculus360
16301 Quorum Dr. Suite 100B
Addison, TX, USA
dbracewell@oculus360.us

Abstract

One way in which marketers gain insights about consumers is by identifying the occasions in which consumers use their products and which are invoked by their products. Identifying occasions helps in consumer segmentation, answering why consumers purchase a product, and where and when they use it. Additionally, the types of occasions a consumer participates in and the social settings surrounding those occasions provide insights into the consumer's personality and sociocultural self. Insights such as these are required for understanding consumer behavior, which marketers need to better design and sell their products. In this paper, we describe a methodology for extracting and categorizing occasions from product reviews, product descriptions, and forum posts. We examine using a maximum entropy markov model (MEMM) and a linear chain conditional random field (CRF) for extraction and find the CRF results in a 72.4% F1-measure. Extracted occasions are categorized as one of six high-level types (*Celebratory*, *Special*, *Seasonal*, *Temporal*, *Weather-Related*, and *Other*) using a support vector machine with an 88.5% macro-averaged F1-measure.

1 Introduction

Social media provides an outlet for consumers to discuss, praise, chastise, and recommend products and services. These consumer generated reviews and commentaries provide marketers insight into the who, what, when, where, why, and how (i.e. the six W's) surrounding the procurement and usage of their products. One way in which marketers answer the six W's is by identifying the occasions, particular times or events, in which their products are used or with which consumers associate their products. These occasions may be routine, e.g. "work" or "at the office", seasonal/weather related, e.g. "rainy day" or "winter", special, e.g. "birthday" or "Christmas", or time related, e.g. "on the run" or "early morning." More than just answering the six W's, occasions also provide a marketer insight into the personality, social status, social circle, and behavior of consumers.

Marketers traditionally rely upon surveys and ethnographic studies in order to gain insights about consumers. The results of these surveys and studies are: (1) consumer segments; (2) when and where the respondents are likely to purchase or use a product; (3) whether they are likely to use the product alone or with others; (4) whether or not the respondents like the product; and (5) are the respondents likely to purchase the product again. These surveys and studies are costly and limited to a much smaller sample size than is obtainable via online reviews and social media. However, current computational approaches to gaining consumer insights typically are limited to the volume and trend of positive and negative comments, reviews, tweets, etc. (Pang et al., 2002; Dini and Mazzini, 2002; Smith et al., 2012; Socher et al., 2013).

Research from the fields of consumer and social psychology, dialogue processing, and affective must be incorporated into computational systems in order for them to replace surveys as a marketer's source of consumer insights. Drawing on these fields of re-

Proceedings of SocialNLP 2015@NAACL-HLT, pages 29–38,
Denver, Colorado, June 5, 2015.

search facilitates an understanding of the attitudes, behaviors, and personal and sociocultural qualities of consumers. Critical to the success of such a computational system is the automated extraction of the occasions in which consumers use a product or with which they associate a product. These occasions and their implicatures provide answers to the six W's and are a basis for understanding a consumer's personal and sociocultural self.

In this paper, we present a methodology for automatically extracting and categorizing occasions in product reviews, product descriptions and forum posts. The extraction of occasions is cast as a sequence labeling problem using the standard BIO encoding. Extracted occasions are categorized as one of six high-level types, *Celebratory*, *Special*, *Seasonal*, *Temporal*, *Weather-Related*, and *Other*, based on common occasions marketers seek to capture in surveys.

2 Related Work

The most related area of research to the extraction of occasions is event extraction. Event extraction deals not only with the extraction of events, but also with the extraction of the entities participating in the events, and other attributes of the event, such as the time (Moschitti et al., 2013), location (Speriosu et al., 2010), and modality (Bracewell et al., 2014). Despite the advances in the extraction of events, the definition of an "event" is ill-defined and changes based on the problem being solved. The Automated Content Extraction (ACE) program defines events using a limited set of types (ACE, 2005). TimeML defines events as "situations that happen or occur" and mainly focuses on the duration properties of the event (Pustejovsky et al., 2003). Instead of precisely defining what an event is, Monahan and Brunson (2014) identify the qualities representative of events.

Research in real-time event detection has benefited from the wide spread acceptance and adoption of social media. Sites like Twitter and Facebook act like social sensors facilitating the real time detection of disasters (Sakaki et al., 2010; Vieweg et al., 2010) and local events (Boettcher and Lee, 2012; Lee and Sumiya, 2010). Relying on the real-time nature of Twitter and the volume of tweets around unusual or significant events, Sakaki et al. (2010) construct a real-time earthquake detection system using twitter users as sensors. Lee and Sumiya (2010) use Twitter to determine unusual local events happening in a given geographic area based on the regularity of tweets against the normal behavior of twitter users in the area.

The dialogue that takes place over social media makes it possible to find and extract life and social events for such purposes as detecting online bullies (Dinakar et al., 2011) and suicide prevention (Jashinsky et al., 2014). Li et al. (2014) target specific replies on Twitter containing manifestations of speech acts, namely congratulations/condolences, to extract major life events, e.g. marriage, using a distant-supervised approach. In addition to the detection of events, work has been done on identifying the social implicatures of dialogue which is in response to a set of events (e.g. Wikipedia page edit) or which may lead to a series events (e.g change in leadership) (Bracewell et al., 2011; Bracewell et al., 2012; Tomlinson et al., 2012).

Broader related research on mining consumer insights is found in the fields of consumer psychology and affective computing. Consumer psychology studies how thoughts, feelings, and perceptions influence the way individuals buy, use, and relate to products, services, and brands. Drawing from other areas in psychology, e.g. social psychology, consumer psychologists formalize the cognitive system of consumers using a categorical representation of products, services, brands and other marketing entities (Loken et al., 2008). Supported by Rosch's (1973) work on prototype theory, Loken and Ward (1990) find a link between the prototypicality of a product and consumers' affect toward it.

A critical component to understanding consumers' affect toward a product is identifying the brands, products, and attributes (or aspects) of the product consumers are mentioning. Wiegand and Klakow (2014) examine separating types from brands, e.g. "soda" vs "coke", using a ranking-based approach which alleviates the need for labeled data. Putthividhya and Hu (2011) use a named entity recognition system to extract product attributes from listing titles on eBay. They focus on extracting brand, style, size, and color within the clothing and shoes categories. Stoica et al. (2007) describe a WordNet-based approach to constructing hierarchical facets relating to aspects associated with a domain or product. Yu et al. (2011) present a domain-assisted approach to constructing aspect hierarchies.

Aspect-based sentiment analysis (Pontiki et al., 2014) merges affect and information extraction seeking to determine the sentiment toward aspects of products, e.g. the consumer sentiment toward the screen of a TV or the food at a restaurant. Approaches to aspect term identification range from standard BIO encoding (Chernyshevich, 2014; Toh and Wang, 2014) to rule-based approaches (Poria et al., 2014). Techniques for aspect polarity detection include machine learning based techniques that integrate multiple sentiment lexicons (Wagner et al., 2014) to grammar based approaches (Brun et al., 2014).

More general than aspect-based sentiment analysis is sentic computing (Cambria and Hussain, 2012). Sentic computing synthesizes common-sense computing, linguistics, and psychology to infer both affective and semantic information about concepts. Cambria et al. (2014) show how SenticNet, a semantic and affective resource, can detect topics and determine polarity in patient opinions.

Another area of research relevant to consumer insights is around the identification of needs and wants on social media. Kanayama and Nasukawa (2008) examine the needs and wants of consumers using syntactic patterns to analyze the demand for products. Ramanand et al. (2010) examine the identification of wishes in reviews and surveys in which consumers make suggestions for improvements and show their intentions to purchase/use a product.

3 Modeling Occasions for Consumer Insights

Occasions are particular times or events and range from the everyday, such as waking up and going to bed, to the special, such as birthdays and weddings. While every occasion is of importance, those surrounding products are of the most use to marketers for gaining insights into consumer behavior. Thus, in this paper we focus only on occasions which are related to a product. More specifically we restrict the definition of an occasion to:

> *Times or happenings in which a product is used or with which a product is associated.*

Occasions matching this definition are in bold font in the following examples:

1. "They are GREAT to take along to a **party** if you're serving crackers and cheese."
2. "I bought these for my **vacation** and they did not disappoint."
3. "Boy, do these take me back to those **misspent days of my foolish youth**."

In the first example the occasion is a party relating to where the reviewer used the product. From this example we can infer that the occasion of use is social, i.e. involved more than just the reviewer, and most probably is informal. Furthermore, we learn that the reviewer believes the product is well suited for party occasions. Given further context about the kind of party, e.g. kids or work, would lead to further insights about the individual, such as if they have children, their age, their occupation, and their marital status. In the second review the occasion ("vacation") is the reason for the reviewer to purchase the product and the answer to when the reviewer used it. Moreover, from the review we can infer that the use of the product was a positive experience for the reviewer. The third review is an example of how a product can be associated with an occasion, which in this case is a memory of the reviewer's youth. Marketers use these type of occasions to connect with consumers at a subconscious and emotional level.

While occasions are closely related to events, not all fit nicely within the ACE and TimeML definitions. For example, take the following:

1. "These boots really kept me warm during the **winter**."
2. "Every time I smell a freshly baked apple pie it **brings me back to my childhood**. "

In the first example the product is a pair of boots and the occasion of use is the winter. Within an event framework winter would not be identified as an event, but as a temporal attribute possibly of a "keep warm". In the second example the occasion is "brings me back to my childhood" and is associated with the product ("apple pie") by the reviewer. The event in the sentence is a "baking" event with

Occasion Type	Definition
Celebratory	Occasions meant to celebrate an event, person, or group of people (e.g. parties and award ceremonies)
Special	Occasions which have significant importance to an individual or group of individuals (e.g. holidays and life events)
Seasonal	Occasions related to the seasons of the year. (e.g. winter)
Weather-Related	Occasions strongly associated with the weather and/or temperature. (e.g. hot days and rainy nights)
Temporal	Occasions tied to a specific time (e.g. 9 to 5, late night, and last year)
Other	Occasions which do not fit in the other categories (e.g. a shopping spree, at the beach)

Figure 1: The six high-level occasion types used to categorize occasion mentions.

the apple pie being the item baked. The occasion is tangential to the event and most likely would not be associated with it by an event extraction system. However, this type of occasion provides evidence of a strong connection between the product and a specific time or event that is nostalgic for the consumer and is invaluable for marketers when crafting their marketing strategy.

Often occasions are associated with special events, such as ceremonies and celebrations. However, as with event types, there are a number of different types of occasions. We define six high-level types, listed in Figure 1, which are based on common occasions marketers use to segment consumers.

Celebratory occasions, which include parties and festivals, are social occasions and inform to the group with which the consumer belongs. An example of a celebratory occasion is:

> "I wore it a couple weeks ago to a **party** and felt festive yet as comfy as if I was wearing loungewear."

Some celebrations are due to special occasions. Special occasions are those which have significant meaning to the consumer, such as holidays and religious observances. The following review excerpt contains mentions of two special occasions:

> "I recommend these for your **engagement party** or **rehearsal dinner**."

Temporal and seasonal occasions relate to the time in which a product is used or associated. An example of a seasonal occasion is :

> "A quintessential style to take you **between seasons**."

The following excerpt from a product description contains two suggested temporal occasions of use:

> "Just the right size for your **day-to-day life**, but elegant enough for **evening**."

Weather-related occasions relate to the weather, e.g. rain and snow, or temperature, e.g. hot and 98 degress. Two examples of weather-related occasions are seen in:

> "The tea is great hot for **chilly nights** and iced for **hot days**."

Finally, we define an other type for occasions that do not neatly fit in one of the previous five categories. An example of an occasion that is marked as other is:

> "Taking a look at the latest summer fashion makes me want to **lie on the beach**."

While there are a multitude of additional occasions types that are definable, we limit the categories to the six presented above in this paper.

4 Data Collection and Annotation

We collect 26,208 sentences from 1,000 product reviews, 500 product descriptions, and 800 forum posts discussing fashion and food related products for annotation. An iterative annotation process is used wherein during each iteration automated machine annotation is performed followed by manual correction. During the initial iteration automated machine annotations are produced using a gazetteer and successive iterations use a machine learning model. Manual correction of the machine annotations involves: (1) removing incorrect occasions; (2) adding missed occasions; and (3) fixing boundaries of partially correct occasions. Due to project constraints all manual correction is performed by one annotator. In the future, we hope to employ multiple annotators.

The initial iteration of the annotation process is performed on 7,000 randomly selected sentences. The gazetteer used during the initial iteration is semi-automatically constructed using WordNet (Miller, 1995). The full hyponym tree and all derivationally related forms for *social event*, *time period*, and the first noun sense of *activity* are extracted to construct the gazetteer.

Examples of occasions identified using the gazetteer are as follows:

1. "Darling **cocktail party** or *date night* dress ."

2. "We only stayed at the **party** an <u>hour</u> because my shoes were killing my feet."

In the examples listed above, occasions in bold font are correctly identified by the gazetteer and left as-is, underlined occasions are incorrectly identified by the gazetteer and removed, and occasions in italic font are not in the gazetteer and added during manual correction. After manual correction (involving the previously three mentioned steps) of the initial 7,000 sentences, 4,500 are randomly selected and held out as test data, and 500 are held out as a development set for occasion extraction. The remaining 2,000 sentences are used as training data for the machine learning model in the second iteration.

The second and successive iterations work on batches of 500 sentences. At each iteration a machine learning model is trained and then used to extract occasions in the new batch of sentences. During each iteration we switch the model we train between the two described in Section 5. We alternate models to ensure we do not bias toward one model and because each model is likely to find something the other did not. The machine identified annotations are manually corrected and added to the set of training data for the next iteration. This process is repeated until all sentences are annotated.

2,393 occasions are annotated across the 26,208 sentences making up the corpus. This an average of 1 occasion every 11 sentences. There is approximately 1 occasion per product review and forum post and 1 occasion every 3 product descriptions.

The next step in the annotation process is to assign a type to each of the 2,393 annotated occasions. We use WordNet to assign an initial type and manually correct the assigned labels. We construct a mapping between WordNet senses and occasion types by starting with a set of twelve seeds, listed in Figure 2. The full hyponym tree and all derivationally related forms of each seed sense are extracted and mapped to the seed's associated occasion type.

WordNet Sense	Occasion Type
party#N#4	Celebratory
celebration#N#1	Celebratory
season#N#2	Seasonal
temperature#N#1	Weather-Related
day#N#1	Temporal
day#N#2	Special
valentine#N#1	Special
gift#N#1	Special
anniversary#N#1	Special
birthday#N#1	Special
special#A#3	Special
New Year#N#1	Special

Figure 2: Seed senses for mapping from WordNet senses to occasions types. Where the sense is described in *lemma#POS#sense* number form.

WordNet lemmas found in a given occasion annotation are examined in right-to-left order. All senses for a lemma are considered in order of sense number. Assignment is performed greedily with the type of the first sense found in the mapping being assigned to the occasion. The *Other* type is assigned if no mapping is found.

Type	Count
Celebratory	107
Seasonal	525
Special	336
Temporal	263
Weather-Related	48
Other	1,114

Table 1: The number of occasions annotated for the six high-level types.

After automatic type assignment is complete the types are manually corrected. Most types are easily determined by an annotator. However, the celebratory and special types do have an overlap, e.g. birthday party. Annotators are told to assign the category of special instead of celebratory when the celebration is associated with a life event (e.g. birthday and engagement parties). The breakdown of the number occasions of each type is shown in Table 1.

5 Computational Methodology and Experimental Results

We divide the extraction and categorization of occasions into two different tasks. We found in preliminary experiments that this division produces better results than jointly performing the two tasks. The rest of this section details the models and results for each task.

5.1 Automatically Extracting Occasions

We model the extraction of occasions using the standard BIO encoding. Words in a sentence are labeled as *B-Occasion*, *I-Occasion*, or *Other* depending on if the word begins an occasion phrase, is within an occasion phrase, or is outside of an occasion phrase respectively. We experiment using a maximum entropy markov model (MEMM) (McCallum et al., 2000) and a linear chain conditional random field (CRF) (Lafferty et al., 2001) to perform extraction. We use an in-house implementation of MEMMs, which uses the LibLinear library (Fan et al., 2008), and CRFsuite (Okazaki, 2007) for the CRF implementation. Parameters are tuned using a grid search to maximize the F1-measure over the 500 sentence development set. The optimal parameters for the MEMM are $C = 3$ and the optimal parameters for the CRF are $C1 = 0$ and $C2 = 2$.

The feature templates used for the extraction of occasions are listed in Figure 3. The features consist of surface, syntactic, and semantic information about the word and its context. Syntactic information is in the form of part-of-speech information and semantic information is in the form of WordNet super sense, i.e. lexicographer filenames (note that all possible super senses are for a word, i.e. no sense disambiguation is performed). These features, with the exception of the WordNet-based feature, are commonly used in other sequence labeling tasks, such as shallow parsing and named entity recognition. We eliminate all features that occur only once in our training set.

Current word	w_i	& t_i
Current word & POS	w_i, p_i	& t_i
Previous word & POS	w_{i-1}, p_{i-1}	& t_i
Word two back & POS	w_{i-2}, p_{i-2}	& t_i
Next word & POS	w_{i+1}, p_{i+1}	& t_i
Word two ahead & POS	w_{i+2}, p_{i+2}	& t_i
Bigram word	w_{i-2}, w_{i-1}	& t_i
	w_{i-1}, w_i	& t_i
	w_i, w_{i+1}	& t_i
	w_{i+1}, w_{i+2}	& t_i
Bigram word & POS	$w_{i-2}, p_{i-2}, w_{i-1}, p_{i-1}$	& t_i
	$w_{i-1}, p_{i-1}, w_i, p_i$	& t_i
	$w_i, p_i, w_{i+1}, p_{i+1}$	& t_i
	$w_{i+1}, p_{i+1}, w_{i+2}, p_{i+2}$	& t_i
Trigram word	w_{i-2}, w_{i-1}, w_i	& t_i
	w_i, w_{i+1}, w_{i+2}	& t_i
Current POS	p_i	& t_i
Previous POS	p_{i-1}	& t_i
POS two back	p_{i-2}	& t_i
Next POS	p_{i+1}	& t_i
POS two ahead	p_{i+2}	& t_i
Bigram POS	p_{i-2}, p_{i-1}	& t_i
	p_{i-1}, p_i	& t_i
	p_i, p_{i+1}	& t_i
	p_{i+1}, p_{i+2}	& t_i
Current word is punct.	$isPunctuation(w_i)$	& t_i
Current word is digit	$isDigit(w_i)$	& t_i
Current word is letter	$isLetter(w_i)$	& t_i
Current word is upper	$isUppercase(w_i)$	& t_i
Current word is lower	$isLowercase(w_i)$	& t_i
WordNet super sense	$ss_{ij} \forall sense(w_i)$	& t_i

Figure 3: Feature templates used for extracting occasions. $w_1, \cdots, w_n$ are the words in the sentence and w_i the current word. $p_1, \cdots, p_n$ is the part-of-speech sequence for the sentence and p_i is the part-of-speech for the current word w_i. $sense(w_i)$ returns all possible senses for the current word, w_i, and ss_{ij} is the super sense associated with sense j. t_i is the tag assigned to the i'th word.

5.1.1 Results

Performance is measured using the CoNLL precision, recall, and F1-measure and the percentage instance error in which an occasion is correct if and only if it exactly matches a gold standard annotation. Results for the MEMM and CRF are listed in Table2. As is in seen in the table, the CRF model outperforms the MEMM with an increase in precision of 4.5%, recall of 20.6%, and F1-measure of 16.5%. Additionally, the CRF has an approximately 57% decrease in instance error rate.

Model	P	R	F1	Err
MEMM	79.2%	43.2%	55.9%	4.9%
CRF	**83.7%**	**63.8%**	**72.4%**	**2.8%**

Table 2: CoNLL **P**recision, **R**ecall, **F1**-measure, and percentage instance **Err**or results for extracting occasions.

Table 3 lists the precision, recall, and F1-measure

by length of the occasion in words. The performance of the MEMM degrades as the length of the occasion increases whereas the performance of the CRF is consistent across the varying lengths. One explanation of why the CRF performs better than the MEMM is the label-bias problem. Label-bias is a known weakness of MEMMs, which CRFs address, in which contextual information is lost around low-entropy transitions due to the use of a per-state (vs single) exponential model (Lafferty et al., 2001).

Model	Length	P	R	F1
MEMM	1	79.8%	55.6%	65.6%
	2	84.6%	41.8%	55.9%
	3	75.0%	25.5%	38.1%
	4	76.9%	35.7%	48.8%
	5+	40.0%	66.7%	11.4%
CRF	1	83.9%	52.8%	64.8%
	2	80.8%	74.6%	77.6%
	3	89.2%	70.2%	78.6%
	4	85.7%	85.7%	85.7%
	5+	80.8%	70.0%	75.0%

Table 3: CoNLL **P**recision, **R**ecall and **F1**-measure by length of occasion in words.

Examples where the CRF and MEMM extract an occasion correctly are:

1. "Just what you need for a **hot summer day**!"
2. "We (my son and I) purchased this gift set for my wife on **Valentines day**."
3. "It's the perfect size to take me from a **day at work** to a **night out for drinks with friends**."

In the first example, the occasion ("hot summer day") is noun phrase representing the reviewer's belief of a good time to use the product. In the second example the occasion is a holiday ("Valentines day"). The final example contains two occasion mentions that represent a time range, in the form of *from* $time_1$ *to* $time_2$.

5.2 Automatically Categorizing Occasions

Once an occasion is extracted it is categorized as one of the previously defined six types. We examine the effectiveness of categorizing occasions given only the occasion and no context. This task is an example of a short-text classification problem (Sriram et al., 2010). To solve this task we use a multi-class support vector machine as implemented in the LibLinear library (Fan et al., 2008). We use the default values for the C and ϵ parameters.

Three features are used for determining the type of an occasion. The first is the standard bag of words with words normalized to lowercase. The second feature is the WordNet super senses of all possible senses found in the occasion. The super senses for adjectives and adverbs in WordNet are not as well defined as they are for nouns and verbs. Because of this, we use the super sense for the associated noun sense using the derivationally related form relation for adjectives and the pertainym (adverb to adjective) and derivationally related form (adjective to noun) relations for adverbs. The final feature is the SUMO concepts (Benzmüller and Pease, 2012) associated with all WordNet senses in the occasion.

5.2.1 Results

Table 4 lists the 10-fold cross-validation results for determining the type of a given occasion. As is seen in the table, F1-measures range from 71.9% for weather-related to 96.7% for seasonal.

Type	P	R	F1
Celebratory	92.6%	84.7%	88.5%
Seasonal	95.9%	97.5%	96.7%
Special	96.5%	93.8%	95.1%
Temporal	80.6%	88.6%	84.4%
Weather-Related	78.0%	66.7%	71.9%
Other	94.5%	93.8%	94.2%
Macro-avg	89.7%	87.5%	88.5%
Micro-avg	93.1%	93.1%	93.1%

Table 4: 10-fold cross-validation **P**recision, **R**ecall, and **F1**-measure for categorizing occasions as *Celebratory, Special, Seasonal, Temporal, Weather-Releated*, or *Other*.

Examples of errors in type assignment are shown in Figure 4. The errors in the first two examples happen due to "spring" and "time" being highly associated with seasonal and temporal occasions respectively. In the third example, the system assigns the type other whereas the true type is special. While the act of "shooting photos" is itself not special the type of photos ("engagement") in the example does make it special. In the fourth example the occasion "upcoming year" is assigned special by the system most likely due to its similarity to the variations of the "new year" special occasions in the corpus. The fi-

Occasion	Gold	System
1.) "new spring semester"	Temporal	Seasonal
2.) "spend time with the one you love"	Other	Temporal
3.) "shooting your engagement photos"	Special	Other
4.) "upcoming year"	Temporal	Special
5.) "Halloween party"	Special	Celebratory

Figure 4: Examples of errors in the assignment of types to occasions.

nal error is a common example of confusion dealing with celebrations taking place as part of a special occasion. The gold standard annotations label these as special occasions whereas the system mostly identifies them as celebratory.

6 Conclusion

In this paper we introduce a methodology for extracting and categorizing occasions in which a product is used or with which a product is associated. We focus primarily on product descriptions, product reviews, and forum posts which are comments or reviews about a product. Occasions are categorized as one of six types: *Celebratory*, *Special*, *Seasonal*, *Temporal*, *Weather-Related*, and *Other*. Extraction and categorization are treated as separate tasks with extraction casted as a BIO encoded sequence labeling problem and categorization as a short text classification problem.

We examine the use of a MEMM and CRF for extracting occasions and find that the CRF model outperforms the MEMM. Categorization is cast as six-class classification problem with a support vector machine used to predict the best type. Categorization results in a macro-averaged F1-measure of 88.5%.

In the future, we plan to identify the relation between products/attributes and occasions and between two occasions. We envision product-occasion relations to include usage and procurement and relations between two occasions to include standard event relations, such as causation. We also plan to increase the amount of training data including multiple new product domains. With the addition of new training data we will also expand upon the current set of six occasions types. In particular, we will examine the use of topic models, such as Latent Dirichlet Allocation, to split the "Other" category into multiple topically relevant ones. We posit that while there exists a set of core occasion categories the vast majority are domain-dependent.

References

ACE. 2005. The ace 2005 (ace05) evaluation plan. http://www.nist.gov/speech/tests/ace/ace05/doc/ace05-evalplan.v3.pdf.

Christoph Benzmüller and Adam Pease. 2012. Higher-order aspects and context in SUMO. *Journal of Web Semantics (Special Issue on Reasoning with context in the Semantic Web)*, 12-13:104–117.

Alexander Boettcher and Dongman Lee. 2012. Eventradar: A real-time local event detection scheme using twitter stream. In *GreenCom'12*, pages 358–367.

David B Bracewell, Marc Tomlinson, Ying Shi, Jeremy Bensley, and Mary Draper. 2011. Who's playing well with others: Determining collegiality in text. In *Semantic Computing (ICSC), 2011 Fifth IEEE International Conference on*, pages 21–26. IEEE.

David B Bracewell, Marc T Tomlinson, Mary Brunson, Jesse Plymale, Jiajun Bracewell, et al. 2012. Annotation of adversarial and collegial social actions in discourse. In *Proceedings of the Sixth Linguistic Annotation Workshop*, pages 184–192. Association for Computational Linguistics.

David B Bracewell, David Hinote, and Sean Monahan. 2014. The author perspective model for classifying deontic modality in events. In *The Twenty-Seventh International Flairs Conference*.

Caroline Brun, Diana Nicoleta Popa, and Claude Roux. 2014. Xrce: Hybrid classification for aspect-based sentiment analysis. In *Proceedings of the 8th International Workshop on Semantic Evaluation (SemEval 2014)*, pages 838–842, Dublin, Ireland, August. Association for Computational Linguistics and Dublin City University.

Erik Cambria and Amir Hussain. 2012. *Sentic computing*. Springer.

Erik Cambria, Daniel Olsher, and Dheeraj Rajagopal. 2014. Senticnet 3: a common and common-sense knowledge base for cognition-driven sentiment analysis. In *Twenty-eighth AAAI conference on artificial intelligence*.

Maryna Chernyshevich. 2014. Ihs r&d belarus: Cross-domain extraction of product features using crf. In *Proceedings of the 8th International Workshop on Semantic Evaluation (SemEval 2014)*, pages 309–313, Dublin, Ireland, August. Association for Computational Linguistics and Dublin City University.

Karthik Dinakar, Roi Reichart, and Henry Lieberman. 2011. Modeling the detection of textual cyberbullying. In *The Social Mobile Web*.

Luca Dini and Giampaolo Mazzini. 2002. Opinion classification through information extraction. In *Proceedings of the Conference on Data Mining Methods and Databases for Engineering, Finance and Other Fields (Data Mining)*, pages 299–310.

Rong-En Fan, Kai-Wei Chang, Cho-Jui Hsieh, Xiang-Rui Wang, and Chih-Jen Lin. 2008. LIBLINEAR: A library for large linear classification. *Journal of Machine Learning Research*, 9:1871–1874.

Jared Jashinsky, Scott H Burton, Carl L Hanson, Josh West, Christophe Giraud-Carrier, Michael D Barnes, and Trenton Argyle. 2014. Tracking suicide risk factors through twitter in the us. *Crisis*.

Hiroshi Kanayama and Tetsuya Nasukawa. 2008. Textual demand analysis: Detection of users' wants and needs from opinions. In *Proceedings of the 22Nd International Conference on Computational Linguistics - Volume 1*, COLING '08, pages 409–416. Association for Computational Linguistics.

John D. Lafferty, Andrew McCallum, and Fernando C. N. Pereira. 2001. Conditional random fields: Probabilistic models for segmenting and labeling sequence data. In *Proceedings of the Eighteenth International Conference on Machine Learning*, ICML '01, pages 282–289, San Francisco, CA, USA. Morgan Kaufmann Publishers Inc.

Ryong Lee and Kazutoshi Sumiya. 2010. Measuring geographical regularities of crowd behaviors for twitter-based geo-social event detection. In *Proceedings of the 2nd ACM SIGSPATIAL international workshop on location based social networks*, pages 1–10. ACM.

Jiwei Li, Alan Ritter, Claire Cardie, and Eduard Hovy. 2014. Major life event extraction from twitter based on congratulations/condolences speech acts. In *Proceedings of the 2014 Conference on Empirical Methods in Natural Language Processing (EMNLP)*, pages 1997–2007, Doha, Qatar, October. Association for Computational Linguistics.

Barbara Loken and James Ward. 1990. Alternative approaches to understanding the determinants of typicality. *Journal of Consumer Research*, pages 111–126.

Barbara Loken, Lawrence W Barsalou, and Christopher Joiner. 2008. Categorization theory and research in consumer psychology. *Handbook of consumer psychology*, pages 133–65.

Andrew McCallum, Dayne Freitag, and Fernando CN Pereira. 2000. Maximum entropy markov models for information extraction and segmentation. In *ICML*, pages 591–598.

George A Miller. 1995. Wordnet: a lexical database for english. *Communications of the ACM*, 38(11):39–41.

Sean Monahan and Mary Brunson. 2014. Qualities of eventiveness. In *Proceedings of the Second Workshop on EVENTS: Definition, Detection, Coreference, and Representation*, pages 59–67, Baltimore, Maryland, USA, June. Association for Computational Linguistics.

Alessandro Moschitti, Siddharth Patwardhan, and Chris Welty. 2013. Long-distance time-event relation extraction. In *Proceedings of the Sixth International Joint Conference on Natural Language Processing*, pages 1330–1338. Asian Federation of Natural Language Processing.

Naoaki Okazaki. 2007. Crfsuite: a fast implementation of conditional random fields (crfs).

Bo Pang, Lillian Lee, and Shivakumar Vaithyanathan. 2002. Thumbs up? Sentiment classification using machine learning techniques. In *Proceedings of the Conference on Empirical Methods in Natural Language Processing (EMNLP)*, pages 79–86.

Maria Pontiki, Dimitris Galanis, John Pavlopoulos, Harris Papageorgiou, Ion Androutsopoulos, and Suresh Manandhar. 2014. Semeval-2014 task 4: Aspect based sentiment analysis. In *Proceedings of the 8th International Workshop on Semantic Evaluation (SemEval 2014)*, pages 27–35, Dublin, Ireland, August. Association for Computational Linguistics and Dublin City University.

Soujanya Poria, Erik Cambria, Lun-Wei Ku, Chen Gui, and Alexander Gelbukh. 2014. A rule-based approach to aspect extraction from product reviews. *SocialNLP 2014*, page 28.

James Pustejovsky, José Castaño, Robert Ingria, Roser Saurí, Robert Gaizauskas, Andrea Setzer, and Graham Katz. 2003. Timeml: Robust specification of event and temporal expressions in text. In *in Fifth International Workshop on Computational Semantics (IWCS-5*.

Duangmanee (Pew) Putthividhya and Junling Hu. 2011. Bootstrapped named entity recognition for product attribute extraction. In *Proceedings of the Conference on Empirical Methods in Natural Language Processing*, EMNLP '11, pages 1557–1567. Association for Computational Linguistics.

J. Ramanand, Krishna Bhavsar, and Niranjan Pedanekar. 2010. Wishful thinking: Finding suggestions and 'buy' wishes from product reviews. In *Proceedings of the NAACL HLT 2010 Workshop on Computational Approaches to Analysis and Generation of Emotion in Text*, CAAGET '10, pages 54–61. Association for Computational Linguistics.

Eleanor H Rosch. 1973. Natural categories. *Cognitive psychology*, 4(3):328–350.

Takeshi Sakaki, Makoto Okazaki, and Yutaka Matsuo. 2010. Earthquake shakes twitter users: real-time event detection by social sensors. In *Proceedings of the 19th international conference on World wide web*, pages 851–860. ACM.

Andrew N Smith, Eileen Fischer, and Chen Yongjian. 2012. How does brand-related user-generated content differ across youtube, facebook, and twitter? *Journal of Interactive Marketing*, 26(2):102–113.

Richard Socher, Alex Perelygin, Jean Wu, Jason Chuang, Christopher D. Manning, Andrew Ng, and Christopher Potts. 2013. Recursive deep models for semantic compositionality over a sentiment treebank. In *Proceedings of the 2013 Conference on Empirical Methods in Natural Language Processing*, pages 1631–1642, Seattle, Washington, USA, October. Association for Computational Linguistics.

Michael Speriosu, Travis Brown, Taesun Moon, Jason Baldridge, and Katrin Erk. 2010. Connecting language and geography with region-topic models. *Models of Spatial Language Interpretation at Spatial Cognition 2010 (COSLI-2010).*, 2010.

Bharath Sriram, Dave Fuhry, Engin Demir, Hakan Ferhatosmanoglu, and Murat Demirbas. 2010. Short text classification in twitter to improve information filtering. In *Proceedings of the 33rd international ACM SIGIR conference on Research and development in information retrieval*, pages 841–842. ACM.

Emilia Stoica, Marti A Hearst, and Megan Richardson. 2007. Automating creation of hierarchical faceted metadata structures. In *HLT-NAACL*, pages 244–251.

Zhiqiang Toh and Wenting Wang. 2014. Dlirec: Aspect term extraction and term polarity classification system. In *Proceedings of the 8th International Workshop on Semantic Evaluation (SemEval 2014)*, pages 235–240, Dublin, Ireland, August. Association for Computational Linguistics and Dublin City University.

Marc T Tomlinson, David B Bracewell, Mary Draper, Zewar Almissour, Ying Shi, and Jeremy Bensley. 2012. Pursing power in arabic on-line discussion forums. In *LREC*, pages 1359–1364.

Sarah Vieweg, Amanda L Hughes, Kate Starbird, and Leysia Palen. 2010. Microblogging during two natural hazards events: what twitter may contribute to situational awareness. In *Proceedings of the SIGCHI Conference on Human Factors in Computing Systems*, pages 1079–1088. ACM.

Joachim Wagner, Piyush Arora, Santiago Cortes, Utsab Barman, Dasha Bogdanova, Jennifer Foster, and Lamia Tounsi. 2014. Dcu: Aspect-based polarity classification for semeval task 4. In *Proceedings of the 8th International Workshop on Semantic Evaluation (SemEval 2014)*, pages 223–229, Dublin, Ireland, August. Association for Computational Linguistics and Dublin City University.

Michael Wiegand and Dietrich Klakow. 2014. Separating brands from types: an investigation of different features for the food domain. In *Proceedings of COLING 2014, the 25th International Conference on Computational Linguistics: Technical Papers*, pages 2291–2302, Dublin, Ireland, August. Dublin City University and Association for Computational Linguistics.

Jianxing Yu, Zheng-Jun Zha, Meng Wang, Kai Wang, and Tat-Seng Chua. 2011. Domain-assisted product aspect hierarchy generation: towards hierarchical organization of unstructured consumer reviews. In *Proceedings of the Conference on Empirical Methods in Natural Language Processing*, pages 140–150. Association for Computational Linguistics.

A Deep Learning and Knowledge Transfer Based Architecture for Social Media User Characteristic Determination

Matthew Riemer, Sophia Krasikov, and Harini Srinivasan
IBM T.J. Watson Research Center
1101 Kitchawan Road
Yorktown Heights, NY 10598, USA
{mdriemer, kras, harini}@us.ibm.com

Abstract

Determining explicit user characteristics based on interactions on Social Media is a crucial task in developing recommendation and social polling solutions. For this purpose, rule based and N-gram based techniques have been proposed to develop user profiles, but they are only fit for detecting user attributes that can be classified by a relatively simple logic or rely on the presence of a large amount of training data. In this paper, we propose a general purpose, end-to-end architecture for text analytics, and demonstrate its effectiveness for analytics based on tweets with a relatively small training set. By performing unsupervised feature learning and deep learning over labeled and unlabeled tweets, we are able to learn in a more generalizable way than N-gram techniques. Our proposed hidden layer sharing approach makes it possible to efficiently transfer knowledge between related NLP tasks. This approach is extensible, and can learn even more from metadata available about Social Media users. For the task of user age prediction over a relatively small corpus, we demonstrate 38.3% error reduction over single task baselines, a total of 44.7% error reduction with the incorporation of two related tasks, and achieve 90.1% accuracy when useful metadata is present.

1 Introduction

Two major Social Media Analytics use cases that are driving business value for businesses today are social recommendation systems and social polling applications.

Social recommendation systems analyze attributes of Social Media users and historical trends to recommend personalized products and advertisements to users. The accuracy and robustness of these systems has a direct impact on user satisfaction and ROI, making improvement of these systems a very worthwhile area of study.

Social polling refers to effectively carrying out massive surveys over Social Media. Organizations find applications with these capabilities useful for brand management, campaign management, and understanding key social trends. State of the art social polling systems include a capability of measuring trending topics and sentiment. These systems also include a capability to analyze the user characteristic level dependencies of these trends. For this use case, informative characteristics for businesses to analyze may include a user's age range, gender, ethnicity, income range, location, hobbies, political leanings, and brand affinities. Additionally, both high precision and high recall for all features is paramount to the success of these systems. Low precision or low recall for user attributes skew trends seen over aggregate data, and defeat the purpose of using these solutions to discover statistically founded business insights.

Social Media organizations, generally with strong inherent privacy restrictions, like Facebook have access to many user level characteristics that have been directly inputted to the website. However, there is great interest in analyzing these same kinds of qualities on more public platforms like Twitter and Blogs, where comments are more rea-

Proceedings of SocialNLP 2015@NAACL-HLT, pages 39–47,
Denver, Colorado, June 5, 2015.

dily accessible to organizations interested in Social Media analytics. In this situation, text analytics techniques are commonly used to infer qualities about these users that are not explicitly provided to organizations analyzing this content.

The difficulty of extracting a characteristic about a user based on tweets alone varies greatly by the type of characteristic. NLP rule based approaches (Krishnamurthy et al., 2009) have been commonly used as a means to perform microsegment analysis of Social Media users. These techniques have been very effective at creating extractors for user attributes like "fan of" relationships, and gender determination with the presence of very little training data. For example, by knowing the key characters, actors, and plot details of a TV show, the logic is intuitive for making an individual rule based extractor that monitors expressed interest by a Social Media user in that show. Moreover, a gender prediction system can be made pretty reliable simply by extracting profile first names, and matching to large lists of female and male names. However, rule based techniques are not good solutions for analyzing more subtle relationships in social posts like those needed for predicting a user's age range, income range, or political leanings. Additionally, as social trends change and users age, it is very desirable for classifiers focused on these tasks to be adaptive and have the ability to efficiently relearn from scratch.

As such, Machine Learning techniques make sense as a means for creating classifiers of more complex user characteristics. N-gram based techniques have commonly been applied to social media analytics problems (Go et al., 2009), (Kökciyan et al., 2013), and (Speriosu et al., 2011). However, we have found that these techniques are not effective without a substantial amount of supervised training data or an extremely reliable semi-supervised method of creating a stand-in corpus.

In this paper, we propose an end-to-end architecture to address the key problems exhibited with common NLP techniques in analyzing subtly expressed social media user characteristics. We will demonstrate our architecture's effectiveness at predicting user age based on a modest 1266 user training set compiled by a team of four researchers in a few hours of work for each person manually annotating data. Our end-to-end method improves on N-gram machine learning techniques by:

1. Building unsupervised text representations that naturally pick up semantic and syntactic synonymy relationships.
2. Effectively utilizing knowledge acquired from unlabelled data.
3. Taking advantage of powerful deep neural networks to increase prediction accuracy.
4. Leveraging a practical framework for transferring knowledge between related user characteristic classifiers for increased performance without increasing the number of free parameters.
5. Establishing a methodology for efficient knowledge transfer from structured metadata related to a user.

Although our main intent is to show the effectiveness of our architecture for Social Media analytics use cases, there is little about our system that has virtues specific to the social media domain. Considering the collection of a user's historical tweets as equivalent to a text document, our approach can serve as a general purpose text analytics architecture, especially for use cases with limited training data. In fact, tweets are generally regarded as more challenging to analyze than other text because of the noisy language and ambiguous content.

The rest of the paper is organized as follows: In Section 2, we describe our data set and go over our experimental methodology. Section 3 gives an overview of the benefits we see by exploring unsupervised text vector techniques. In Section 4 we explain the benefit of building deep learning models on top of unsupervised features. We proceed to explain popular multitask deep learning techniques and their failures for our problem statement in Section 5. Section 6 is an overview of our hidden layer sharing approach, which we validate in Section 7. Section 8 explains how our model is extensible for the incorporation of structured metadata. Finally, Section 9 concludes the paper.

2 Experimental Methodology

Without access to any reliable user provided age information, we had to rely on human judgment to create gold standard annotations for the ages of users on Twitter. We randomly generated Twitter usernames and had a team of four people manually go to Twitter.com and look at their profile. The instructions were to look at the user's Twitter profile including pictures and their tweets to judge their age range and discard any users for whom the age range was not clear. The annotators looked through the user's recent tweets to validate their age and also annotated with gender and ethnicity where possible. Each user in our dataset was analyzed by two different annotators, and only those in which there was agreement for all characteristics were kept. Ultimately, we compiled a dataset of 1808 annotated Twitter profiles, and retrieved historical tweets from their accounts. Depending on individual usage patterns, we retrieved a very variable number of tweets. The minimum was 5, the maximum was 7115, the average was 226.6, the median was 96, and the standard deviation was 326.

Age Range	Training Count	Test Count
Generation Y	590	253
Generation X	352	152
Older	323	138

Table 1: Total counts of the annotated Twitter users in our training set and test set by age range.

For our first attempt to create an age prediction system, we attempted to use rules. However, we quickly found that even things like usage of currently trending slang were not reliable in predicting age groups. Moreover, rule based systems did not seem to have the potential to achieve even modest recall. Clearly, age prediction could not be accurately performed deterministically based on tweets, and a technique that used a complex evidence based model would be needed.

Our second attempt at age prediction then was to use popular machine learning text analytics models based on N-grams. We deployed these models using classifiers in the NLTK python package (Bird et al., 2009). We tried Naïve Bayes, and Maximum Entropy models for unigrams, bigrams, and trigrams. We found that it was optimal to require a minimum of 3 training corpus occurrences for an N-gram to be included in our feature space.

Description	GenY-F1	GenX-F1	Older-F1
1-Gram ME	69.5	17.3	38.4
2-Gram ME	69.5	17.3	38.4
3-Gram ME	66.6	13.0	24.5
1-Gram NB	73.0	36.1	18.3
2-Gram NB	73.0	36.1	18.3
3-Gram NB	72.6	33.2	23.6

Table 2: F1 scores by age range category for Naïve Bayes and Maximum Entropy unigram, bigram, and trigram models.

Table 2 depicts the test set results from our Maximum Entropy and Naïve Bayes analysis. Increasing the our granularity to include bigrams and trigrams resulted in an better training set performance for Maximum Entropy and Naïve Bayes, but those increases did not generalize to the test set. Maximum Entropy models saw degradation in accuracy with higher level N-grams. For Naïve Bayes, there was a slight improvement based on an increase in performance at predicting the oldest age range. Regardless, these results would not be suitable for a deployed system to make confident judgments.

As we began exploring other techniques which we will describe in more detail in subsequent sections, we use Paragraph Vector as provided by the original developers (Mesnil et al., 2015). Additionally, we used the theano-hf python package (Boulanger-Lewandowski et al., 2012) as the beginning building block for our deep learning based approaches.

3 Unsupervised Text Vectors

Neural Network Language Models (NNLMs) were first proposed by (Bengio et al., 2001), and have since become a major focus of research in building feature representations for text. (Mikolov et al., 2013), (Pennington et al., 2014), and (Levy and Goldberg, 2014) demonstrate that high quality vectors mapping N-gram phrases to latent vectors can be learned over large amounts of unlabelled data. These vectors have been shown to be able to naturally express synonymy through vector similarity and relationships through vector arithmetic. From a practical perspective, this work can be very useful to systems with limited training data as unlabelled public data is readily available, while supervised labeled training data often is not.

	Training				Testing			
Description	Accuracy	GenY-F1	GenX-F1	Older-F1	Accuracy	GenY-F1	GenX-F1	Older-F1
3-Gram ME	**87.3**	**88.1**	**82.9**	**90.0**	51.9	66.6	13.0	24.5
3-Gram NB	84.5	85.7	81.6	84.7	**56.4**	72.6	**33.2**	23.6
PV Logistic Regression	57.2	73.0	32.7	49.7	56.2	**72.8**	30.6	**46.9**

Table 3: Accuracies and F1 scores by age prediction category for Paragraph Vector (PV), Maximum Entropy (ME), and Naïve Bayes (NB) models.

In this paper we use Paragraph Vector, proposed by (Le & Mikolov, 2014), to build unsupervised language models. The key idea of this model is to predict nearby words with a fixed context window of surrounding words. Paragraph Vector extends to any segment of text with any length by allowing each unit of text (i.e. units in our experiments are a group of historical tweets for a particular user) to be represented by its own vector that is learned by contributing to the prediction of nearby words along with the words in the context window. Paragraph Vector has been shown to be a state of the art technique for analyzing supervised document level sentiment. However, we envision our end-to-end architecture as not being tied to a particular unsupervised feature learning technique. In fact, the drawback of Paragraph Vector is that all text units must be stored in memory, and an iterative inference step is needed during runtime. Eventually it is not unlikely that advances and variation in Recurrent Neural Network Language Models, as discussed in (Mikolov et al., 2010) and (Sutskever et al., 2011), or Recursive Neural Networks, as in (Socher et al., 2013) and (Socher et al., 2011), will provide a more scalable alternative for mapping text segments of arbitrary length to vectors.

In this section we will explore the performance of the unsupervised text vector component of our end-to-end architecture. We will first discuss the comparison between the unmodified Paragraph Vector method and popular N-gram machine learning models. Then we will discuss the effect of augmenting Paragraph Vector with unlabelled data.

3.1 Comparison with N-gram Models

In this experiment we implemented Naïve Bayes and Maximum Entropy N-gram models to serve as machine learning baselines over our age prediction dataset. We trained Paragraph Vector with a word context window of 8, 20 training epochs, and text vectors of length 300. After establishing text vectors for the training set of user tweet collections, we trained a logistic regression classifier as (Le & Mikolov, 2014) do in their original sentiment analysis paper.

Table 3 displays the results of this analysis. When it comes to testing accuracies and age range specific F1 scores, Paragraph Vector seems to result in the most well rounded representation, but the Naïve Bayes trigram model actually achieves a slightly higher overall accuracy. However, one clearly evident differentiator between the techniques can be seen in the breakdown of the results over the training set.

The trigram Maximum Entropy model experiences a 35.4% drop-off in accuracy from the training set to the test set, Naïve Bayes experiences a 28.1% drop-off in accuracy, and Paragraph Vector only falls 1%. It seems as though particularly for the case of the tougher Generation X and Older ranges, the N-gram models overfit on this small training set in a way that does not generalize. The Paragraph Vector model, however, has built a notion of text synonym that constricts its learning to knowledge that will generalize. Table 3 seems to indicate that despite similar performance, the Paragraph Vector model has a far better idea of its own true accuracy than N-gram models and has the potential at least to significantly improve whereas the N-gram models are much closer to their accuracy limitations given the small training dataset.

3.2 Knowledge Transfer From Unlabelled Data

In order to extend the Paragraph Vector model, we explored the possibility of expanding its knowledge coverage by incorporating unlabelled data. As we were concerned about the effect on performance of both storing and conducting inference over text segment vectors at scale, we did not include any additional user profile vectors in our model. Instead, additional unlabelled tweets were added to the Paragraph Vector training and only the words were considered.

	Testing			
Logistic Regression	Accuracy	GenY-F1	GenX-F1	Older-F1
Age Corpus	56.2	72.8	30.6	46.9
Age Corpus + 1 Million Tweets	61.3	**78.2**	35.6	53.0
Age Corpus + 10 Million Tweets	**63.2**	77.9	**42.0**	**53.4**

Table 4: Logistic regression Paragraph Vector results with the incorporation of additional text.

Table 4 shows that as more tweets are included, the Paragraph Vector model becomes better. In fact, the addition of 10 million unlabelled tweets results in a 12.5% relative improvement in the accuracy of the original Paragraph Vector model. It should be noted that each of these corpuses was analyzed over 20 training epochs of Paragraph Vector. It is also important to note at this stage that we have found that the number of training epochs has a big impact on the quality of the text vectors produced by Paragraph Vector. The implication being that training on massive corpuses only makes sense if the time is allotted for a significant number of iterations.

4 Learning Deep Neural Networks from Unsupervised Text Feature Vectors

A logical first step in building powerful representations on top of unsupervised text vectors is to analyze the performance differences between logistic regression and generic deep neural network architectures. 3.03 million total free parameters is a good number that we established as the desired size for our neural network architecture. In these experiments (and all that follow) we kept that size constant across different numbers of hidden layers and every hidden layer was set to be the same size within an individual single task network.

We also restricted our analysis to Paragraph Vector with 10 million unlabelled tweets because it achieves the best performance with logistic regression. Our neural network leverages the Hessian Free Optimizer (Martens, 2010) and (Martens and Sutskever, 2011) in order to traverse pathological curvatures in the error function. We found this method to be considerably better than straightforward stochastic gradient descent in practice. Additionally, our deep neural network was initialized with greedy layer wise pretraining (Hinton et al., 2006). We used sigmoid activation units, a preconditioner, and a cross entropy loss function.

Our deep learning results are depicted in Table 5. Our network increase in performance as we increase the number of hidden layers until hitting a maximum total accuracy of 73.1% with three hidden layers. The three hidden layer network is the most efficient in its use of free parameters, and shines above the rest due to a considerable separation from the pack in predicting Generation X Twitter users – the toughest age range to predict.

		Testing			
# Hidden Layers	# Free Parameters	Accuracy	GenY-F1	GenX-F1	Older-F1
1	3.03M	71.1	87.3	46.4	63.6
2	3.03M	71.6	**88.2**	46.3	62.7
3	3.03M	**73.1**	87.5	**58.3**	66.2
4	3.03M	72.7	87.8	50.4	65.2
5	3.03M	72.0	87.1	46.7	**66.7**

Table 5: Results for different numbers of equal sized hidden layers with a fixed total parameter size.

5 Deep Multitask Learning Architectures

Multitask learning across deep neural network architectures is far from a new idea. The architecture portrayed in Figure 1, taken from (Socher and Manning, 2013), is seemingly of general consensus in the deep learning community (Bengio et al., 2013). The main idea is that a shared input is sent to an arbitrary amount of Neural Network hidden layers that are shared between related tasks and then classified by an arbitrary number of task specific Neural Network hidden layers and a task specific output layer.

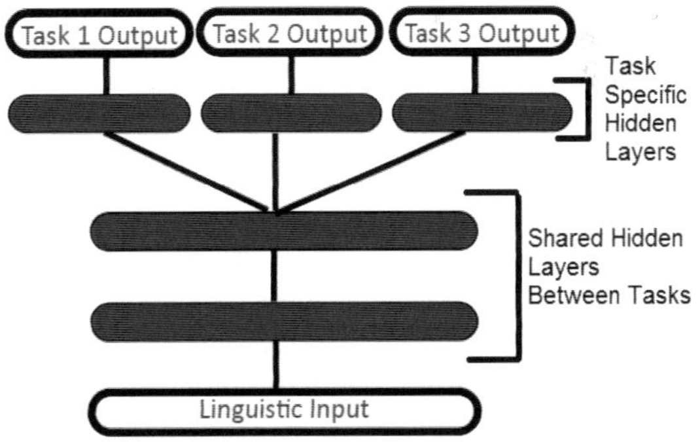

Figure 1: Standard Deep Multitask Learning Architecture Diagram

In (Collobert & Weston, 2008) this general architecture is extended in an attempt to perform Semantic Role Labeling and an unsupervised language model is used to initialize word vectors. However, it is important to note that they have many more training examples in their experiments than we do. In a situation where there is a relatively small number of training examples, we believe it makes more sense to treat unsupervised text mappings as an input feature space for training that is shared across tasks (as opposed to just an initialized layer). Although feature spaces created by unsupervised learning could contain errors, with limited training examples algorithms cannot afford to perform sparse updates based on individual N-grams. It is imperative in learning relationships that generalize well and do not overfit to associate discoveries about phrases with synonyms and phrases of similar meaning. As we have already shown, doing this with high quality unsupervised feature vectors constrains the space of learning and prevents supervised machine learning algorithms from reading too much into misleading co-occurances present in smaller datasets.

A very simple paradigm of multi-task learning can be achieved by concatenating the output for each task and learning a single neural network that simultaneously classifies all tasks. Interestingly, this paradigm resulted in a consistent slight performance degradation in our experiments over single tasks. It seems like adding the extra output indicators must be complicating the process of minimizing error despite more information, even considering the small training corpus. Additionally, this method is only possible for training data that is jointly labeled, which significantly limits it applicability as a technique and seems inconsistent with the individual attention humans successfully exhibit when learning new skills. This limitation motivates the general architecture of Figure 1, which has no requirement for jointly labelled training data.

However, in the general multi-task deep learning model depicted in Figure 1, it is not clear how to approach the order of training tasks. In an extreme example, if you imagine first training one task for all epochs and then training another for all epochs, the first task would essentially serve as an initialization of the base network close to the input that will eventually get very much customized for the second task after enough iterations. We did not find this technique useful in our experiments. In fact, it seems like we may be relatively far from realizing the totality of the apparent promise of multi-task learning with an architecture in the form of Figure 1. In our experiments, we found that training a framework of that form by alternating between tasks every epoch (and even in mini-batches) actually resulted in a degradation of performance over single task learning. In fact, in (Collobert & Weston, 2008), where they loop through tasks in alternating order and update one random training example at a time, the authors find that Semantic Role Labeling is performed better over a large corpus just with Language Model initialization than it is with the additional contributions of knowledge of Part of Speech Tagging, Chunking, and Named Entity Recognition. This result is quite unintuitive given how related these tasks are, and points to a similar phenomenon to what we saw in implementing this paradigm.

6 Hidden Layer Sharing

Our proposed approach to multitask learning is performed with the following procedure:

1. Linguistic input is mapped to a shared unsupervised layer that serves as the effective input feature space for subsequent classifiers.
2. Each task is trained as its own deep neural network – the size of which is specified as a parameter of the model.
3. The output layer of each model is discarded and the top hidden layers for each model are concatenated.
4. The concatenated hidden layers are treated as a new input feature space to subsequent deep neural networks trained for each task. In our experiments we found a one layer logistic regression network with no additional hidden layers to make optimal use of free parameters, but this effect may change for different domains.

Figure 2 depicts an example architecture for hidden layer sharing between two tasks. In contrast to Figure 1, Figure 2c only illustrates classification of a single output at a time. This serves to underscore a critical practical point about prioritization.

In practice the number of free parameters is a constrained value for a production NLP system. We expect machine learning models to increase in performance with an increase in free parameters. On the other hand, there are practical limits

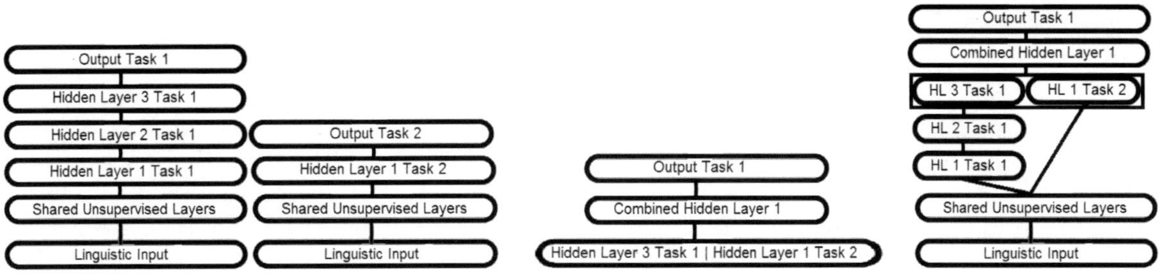

A) Deep Neural Networks are trained seperately for each task.

B) The top hidden layers for each task are concatenated and treated as input to another deep neural network optimized for the main task.

C) The components from A and B are deployed together in a single architecture.

Figure 2: An example of the process and final deployment architecture for our hidden layer sharing approach. Task 1 is the main task to optimize. In this configuration, Task 1 is allotted three task specific hidden layers, Task 2 is allotted one task specific hidden layer, and the network that processes the output from the combined hidden layers in A is allotted one hidden layer on top of the combined input. The logical flow of steps goes from A to B for training and C for deployment. Optionally, fine-tuning can be conducted with the architecture in C.

imposed by the direct relationship between increasing the number of free parameters, increasing a model's memory footprint, and decreasing its runtime throughput. That being said, given the modern hardware these systems are deployed on today, most models hit a point of diminishing returns where increasing parameters has less and less impact on the model's accuracy. As such, the practical promise of multitask learning and knowledge transfer techniques today is to achieve a lift in predictive performance of models while staying constant at the allowable limit for total free parameters. When viewed in this way, it is clear that when considered as the main task being optimized, Task 1 would probably benefit from a different split of free parameters than Task 2 in Figure 2. All else being equal, although Task 2 is useful for improving Task 1, it is not as mission critical as the main task, so Task 1 likely should have more dedicated free parameters than Task 2 if you are classifying Task 1. The reverse would be true if you were classifying Task 2.

In our experiments we see two major positive effects of the hidden layer sharing technique. First, training the models separately seems to allow for a more stable learning for each task that overcomes early local minimums hit by other common architecture types. Second, the ability to directly specify the number of free parameters allocated to each model in early layers results in an ability to tune models for optimal prioritization of related tasks.

7 Measuring The Effectiveness of Hidden Layer Sharing

As discussed in Section 6, a key aspect of our hidden layer sharing approach is the ability to directly adjust the prioritization of tasks. For the case of training age prediction alongside the gender prediction task, we saw significant gains by limiting the amount of parameters in the model allocated to gender prediction. Training the model with a 50-50 split in free parameters allocated between tasks resulted in 68.9% total accuracy (a net decrease in performance from single task results), however, a 70-30 split in favor of the age prediction task brought total accuracy to 73.3%. A 90-10 split achieved the best two task result with 75.0% total accuracy. For the case of training age prediction alongside the ethnicity prediction task, we saw the opposite relationship. When the ethnicity learning task wasn't given enough stake in the shared hidden layer at a 90-10 free parameter split, it hurt our predictive accuracy by bringing it down to 70.7%. However, at an even 50-50 split the ethnicity task free parameters helped age prediction learning enough to overcome our 3 hidden layer single task result by achieving 73.9% total accuracy.

	Testing			
Description	Accuracy	GenY-F1	GenX-F1	Older-F1
3-Gram NB	56.4	72.6	33.2	23.6
PV Logistic Regression	56.2	72.8	30.6	46.9
PV Logistic Regression + 10M Tweets	63.2	77.9	42.0	53.4
3 Hidden Layer NN	73.1	87.5	58.3	66.2
3 Hidden Layer + Gender	75.0	87.6	58.3	**66.9**
3 Hidden Layer + Gender + Ethnicity	**75.9**	**89.4**	**59.9**	62.4

Table 6: Top results with a constrained free parameter size at different architecture points.

Table 6 highlights our best result, which came from integrating a scaled down version of the three hidden layer model with enough free parameters left over to give ethnicity and gender each an equal 10% of the total free parameter stake in the model. A logistic regression layer was built on top of the concatenated shared hidden layers to create a final output. 75.9% total accuracy constitutes a 3.8% relative improvement over deep learning models due to knowledge transfer from two related tasks and a 34.6% relative accuracy improvement over the best performing baseline N-gram model. The hidden layer sharing approach was capable of integrating both gender and ethnicity detection as related tasks to age detection for significant additional gains on top of the large gains resulting from building deep learning on top of unsupervised language model feature vectors. This is a phenomenon that was expected, but not achieved with concatenated output and joint learning driven shared hidden layer architectures.

8 Extensibility of Architecture to Incorporate Available Metadata

Details	# Free Parameters	Accuracy	GenY-F1	GenX-F1	Older-F1
1 Hidden Layer	3.03M	71.1	87.3	46.4	63.6
3 Hidden Layers	3.03 M	**73.1**	87.5	**58.3**	66.2
1 Hidden Layer with Gender	3.03M	81.0	88.2	64.7	82.8
3 Hidden Layers with Gender	3.03M	86.6	88.0	76.4	93.9
1 Hidden Layer with Gender and Ethnicity	3.03M	88.6	89.5	78.1	**97.5**
3 Hidden Layers with Gender and Ethnicity	3.03M	**90.1**	**89.6**	**82.4**	97.5

Table 7: Comparison of results in age range prediction between neural network architectures with a fixed parameter size that are given gender and ethnicity information as structured metadata.

Beyond being able to leverage knowledge from multiple related learned tasks, it is important for a social media analytics solution to be able to properly leverage structured metadata when available. To showcase the ease in which a model in our architecture could do this, we ran an experiment assuming that gender and ethnicity are always given as metadata to our system. In this case we can see in Table 7 that both a single hidden layer model and multiple hidden layer models can benefit significantly from additional structured input that is concatenated with the input unsupervised language model feature vectors. Our 3 hidden layer model from before is able to efficiently incorporate in this structured data for 23.2% relative improvement over the same single task model. This is a very encouraging result to achieve 90.1% total accuracy with such a small age related training set.

The 14.2% gap between our hidden layer sharing result and what is possible with direct knowledge of the same tasks as metadata points out that if we had more training data on related tasks such as gender and ethnicity, it should be possible to achieve high accuracy results without the need for the metadata being directly given. Limitations in accuracy increases resulting from knowledge transfer are at least in part due to the limited accuracy for the individual gender and ethnicity tasks in our current experiments, which are learned over the same small dataset used for age prediction.

9 Conclusion and Future Work

Prediction tasks like age prediction based solely on historical tweets from a user are not possible using rule based techniques and are not possible with limited training data for N-gram machine learning techniques. In this paper, we have shown that using modern machine learning techniques such as the addition of unlabelled training data, deep learning, and knowledge transfer between related tasks, it is possible to achieve 75.9% predictive accuracy with limited training data. In fact, we have shown that these models are very extensible and achieve 86.6% accuracy for the common case where gender is known. Moreover, we can achieve 90.1% predictive accuracy when other useful metadata like ethnicity is present.

In this paper we have proposed a text analytics process flow and hidden layer sharing architecture suitable for solving tough prediction problems on noisy social media text. However, our approach in this paper can be translated to other even seemingly unrelated domains as well, such as business to business lead prediction, which will be the focus of future publications. Our hidden layer sharing approach gives developers the power to specify how a deep neural network stores and prioritizes knowledge between related tasks, where popular techniques generally allow the neural network to figure this out.

The success of this approach points out the need for improvement of shared hidden layer deep neural network approaches which in some cases have a difficult time prioritizing effectively and balancing learning across multiple complex error functions. Additionally, the huge improvements we see with direct knowledge of structured metadata are indicative of the potential that multitask architectures have for classification problems in the social media domain with limited training data.

References

Yoshua Bengio, Réjean Ducharme, and Pascal Vincent. 2001. A Neural Probabilistic Language Model. *Advances in Neural Information Processing Systems '2000,* pages 932-938.

Yoshua Bengio, Aaron Courville, and Pascal Vincent. 2013. Representation learning: A review and new perspectives. *Pattern Analysis and Machine Intelligence, IEEE Transactions on* 35, no. 8, pages 1798-1828.

Steven Bird, Edward Loper, and Ewan Klein. 2009. Natural Language Processing with Python. *O'Reilly Media Inc.*

N. Boulanger-Lewandowski, Y. Bengio and P. Vincent. 2012. Modeling Temporal Dependencies in High-Dimensional Sequences: Application to Polyphonic Music Generation and Transcription. *In Proceedings of ICML*, page 29.

Ronan Collobert, and Jason Weston. 2008. A unified architecture for natural language processing: Deep neural networks with multitask learning. In *Proceedings of the 25th international conference on Machine learning*, pages 160-167.

Alec Go, Richa Bhayani, and Lei Huang. 2009. Twitter sentiment classification using distant supervision. *CS224N Project Report, Stanford*, pages 1-12.

Geoffrey Hinton, Simon Osindero, and Yee-Whye Teh. 2006. A fast learning algorithm for deep belief nets. *Neural computation* 18, no. 7, pages 1527-1554.

Nadin Kökciyan, Arda Celebi, Arzucan Ozgür, and Suzan Usküdarlı. 2013. Bounce: Sentiment classification in Twitter using rich feature sets. In *Second Joint Conference on Lexical and Computational Semantics (* SEM)*, vol. 2, pages 554-561.

Rajasekar Krishnamurthy, Yunyao Li, Sriram Raghavan, Frederick Reiss, Shivakumar Vaithyanathan, and Huaiyu Zhu. 2009. SystemT: a system for declarative information extraction. *ACM SIGMOD Record* 37, no. 4, pages 7-13.

Quoc Le, and Tomas Mikolov. Distributed Representations of Sentences and Documents. 2014. In *Proceedings of the 31st International Conference on Machine Learning (ICML-14)*, pages 1188-1196.

Omer Levy, and Yoav Goldberg. Neural word embedding as implicit matrix factorization. 2014. In *Advances in Neural Information Processing Systems*, pages 2177-2185.

James Martens. Deep learning via Hessian-free optimization. 2010. In *Proceedings of the 27th International Conference on Machine Learning (ICML-10)*, pages 735-742.

James Martens, and Ilya Sutskever. 2011. Learning recurrent neural networks with hessian-free optimization. In *Proceedings of the 28th International Conference on Machine Learning (ICML-11)*, pages 1033-1040.

Grégoire Mesnil, Tomas Mikolov, Marc'Aurelio and Yoshua Bengio. 2015. Ensemble of Generative and Discriminative Techniques for Sentiment Analysis of Movie Reviews. Submitted to the *workshop track of ICLR 2015.*

Tomas Mikolov, Martin Karafiát, Lukas Burget, Jan Cernocký, and Sanjeev Khudanpur. Recurrent neural network based language model. 2010. In *INTERSPEECH 2010, 11th Annual Conference of the International Speech Communication Association, Makuhari, Chiba, Japan, September 26-30, 2010*, pages 1045-1048.

Tomas Mikolov, Ilya Sutskever, Kai Chen, Greg S. Corrado, and Jeff Dean. Distributed representations of words and phrases and their compositionality. 2013. In *Advances in Neural Information Processing Systems*, pages 3111-3119.

Jeffrey Pennington, Richard Socher, and Christopher D. Manning. 2014. Glove: Global vectors for word representation. In *Proceedings of the Empiricial Methods in Natural Language Processing (EMNLP 2014)* page 12.

Michael Speriosu, Nikita Sudan, Sid Upadhyay, and Jason Baldridge. 2011. Twitter polarity classification with label propagation over lexical links and the follower graph. In *Proceedings of the First workshop on Unsupervised Learning in NLP*, pages 53-63. Association for Computational Linguistics.

Richard Socher, Christopher D. Manning, and Andrew Y. Ng. Learning continuous phrase representations and syntactic parsing with recursive neural networks. 2010. In *Proceedings of the NIPS-2010 Deep Learning and Unsupervised Feature Learning Workshop*, pages 1-9.

Richard Socher, and Chrisopher Manning. 2013. Deep Learning for Natural Language Processing (without Magic). 2013. Tutorial at *NAACL HLT 2013.*

Richard Socher, Alex Perelygin, Jean Y. Wu, Jason Chuang, Christopher D. Manning, Andrew Y. Ng, and Christopher Potts. 2013. Recursive deep models for semantic compositionality over a sentiment treebank. In *Proceedings of the conference on empirical methods in natural language processing (EMNLP)*, vol. 1631, pages 1642.

Ilya Sutskever, James Martens, and Geoffrey E. Hinton. 2011. Generating text with recurrent neural networks. In *Proceedings of the 28th International Conference on Machine Learning (ICML-11)*, pages 1017-1024.

Author Index